This Coloring Book Belongs To:

____

____

Color Chart

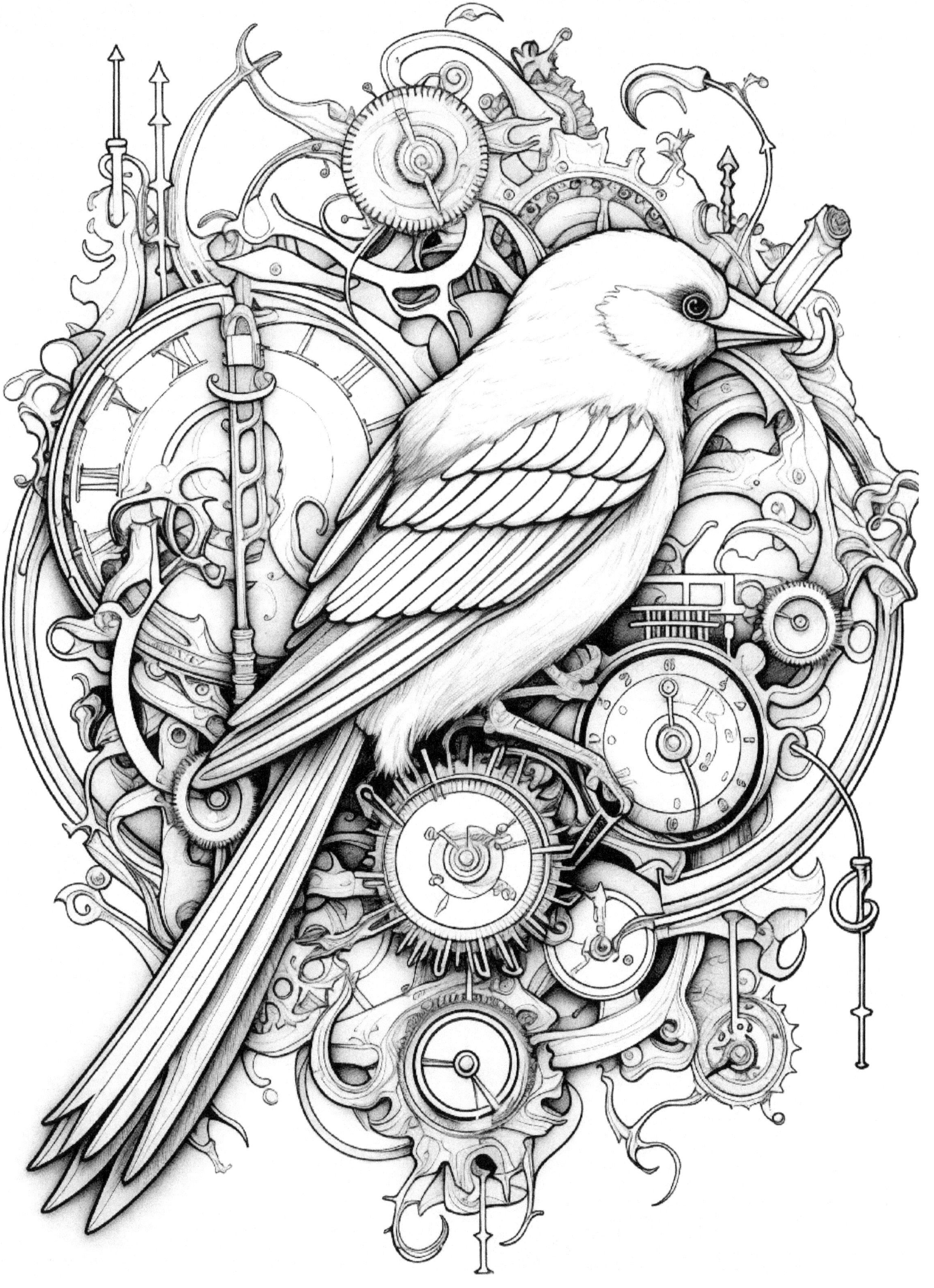

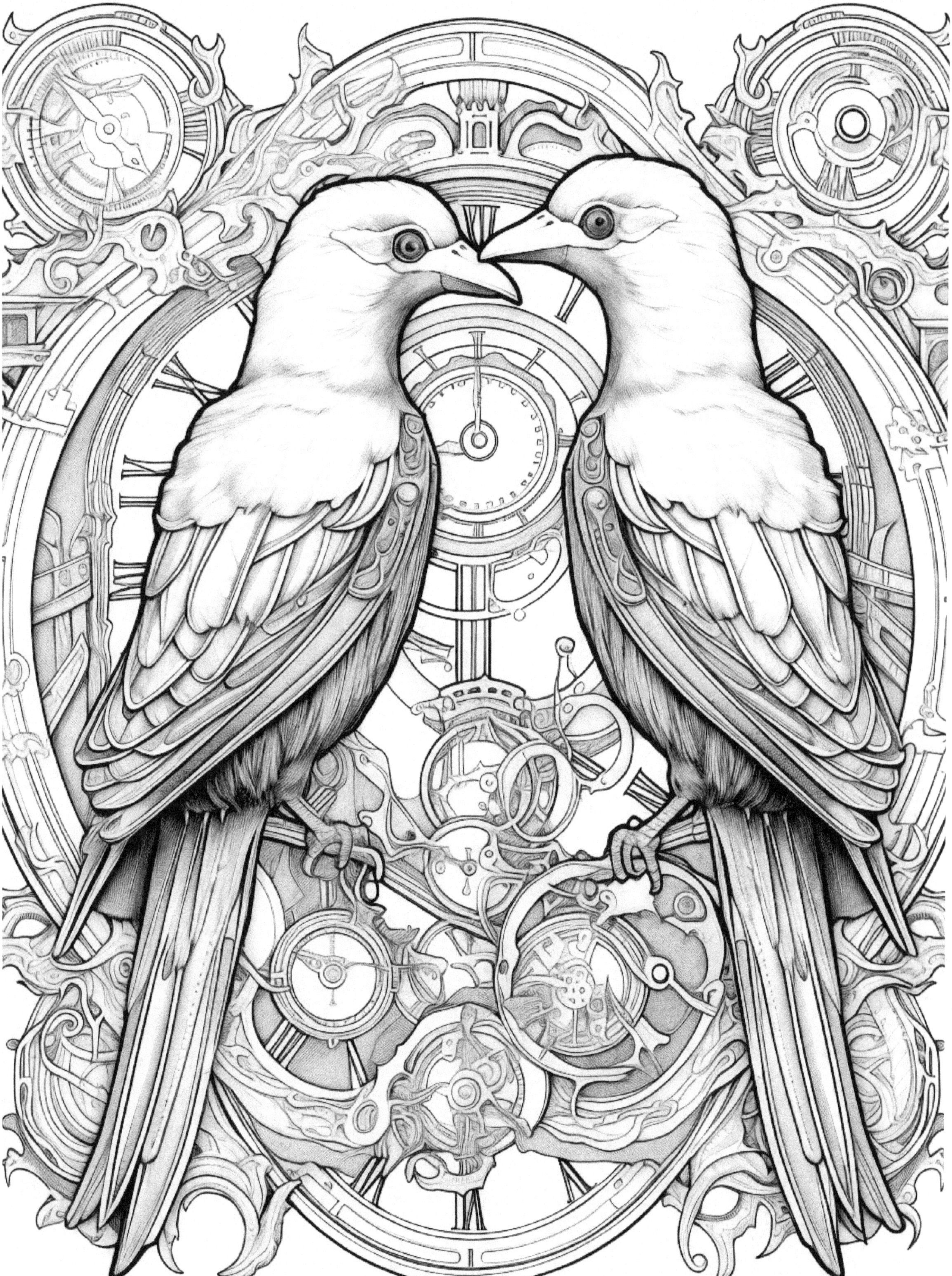

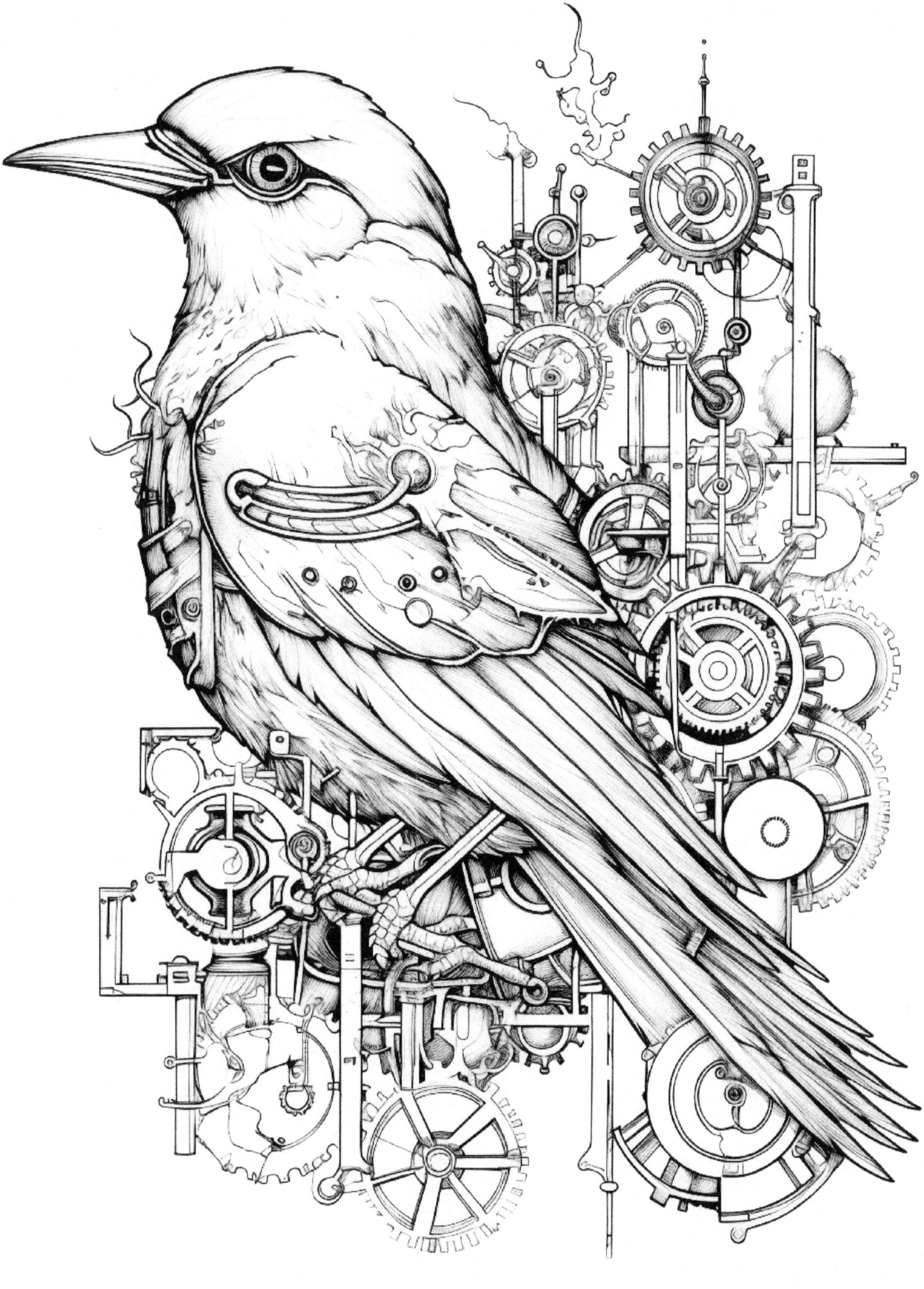

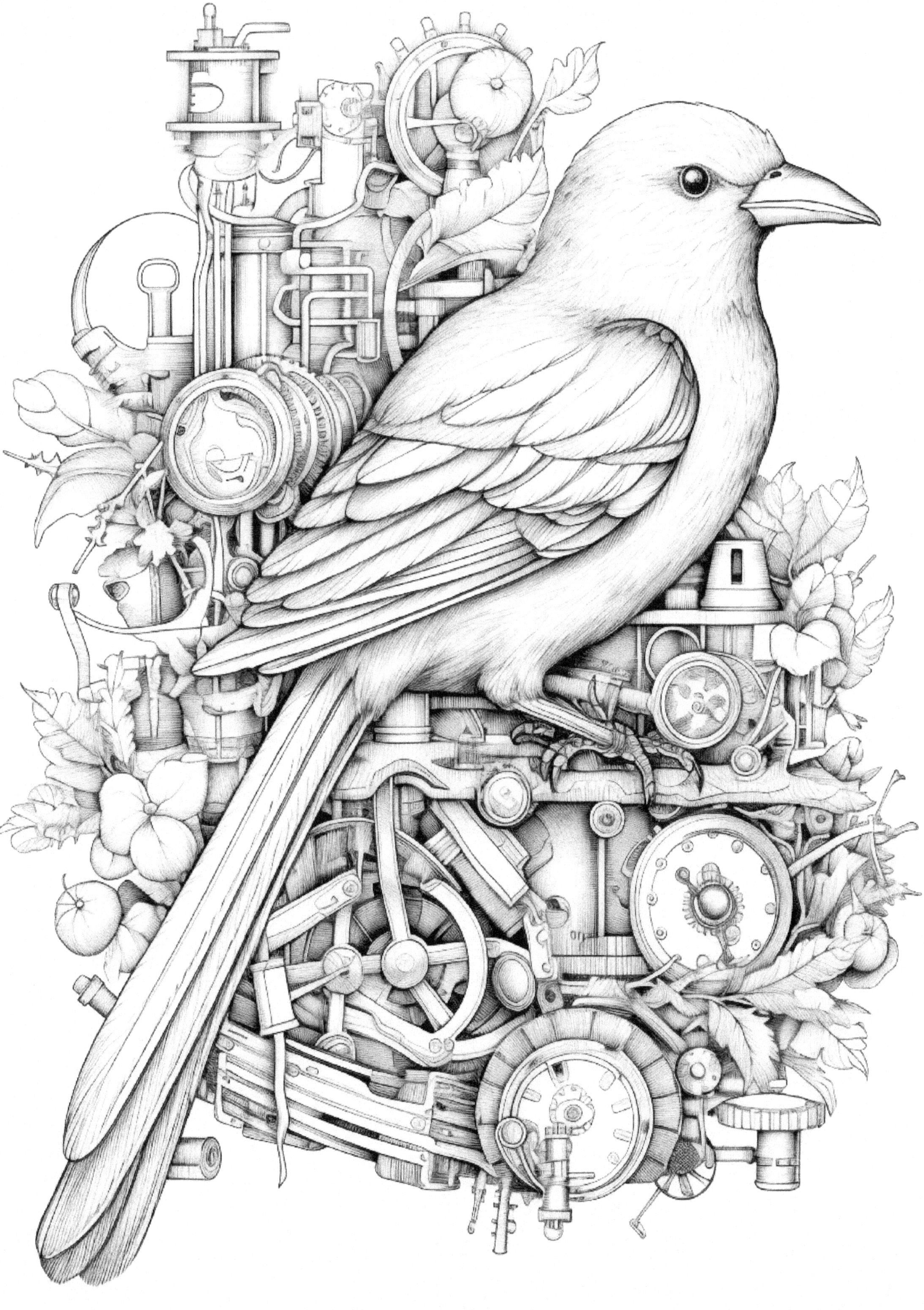

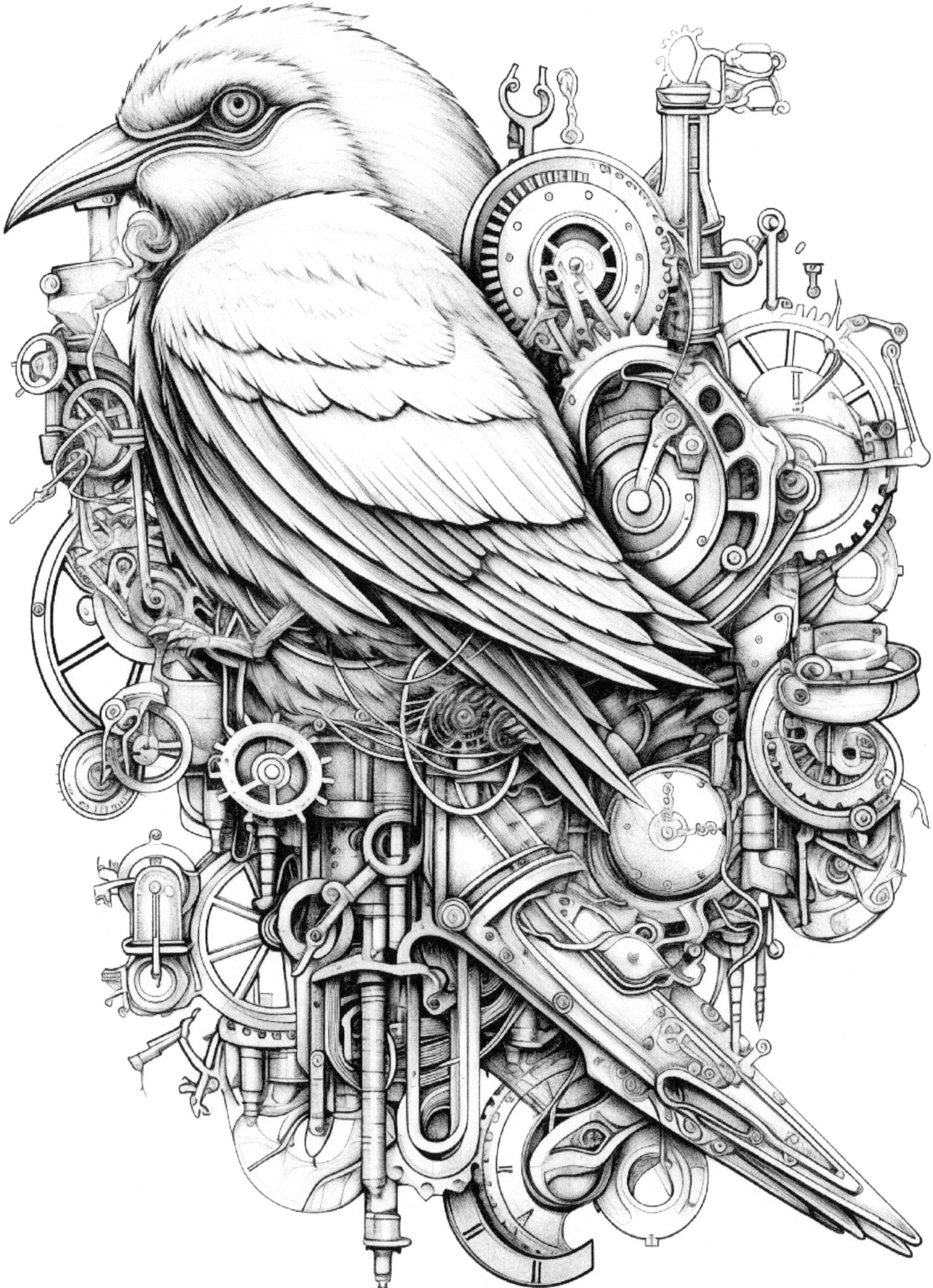

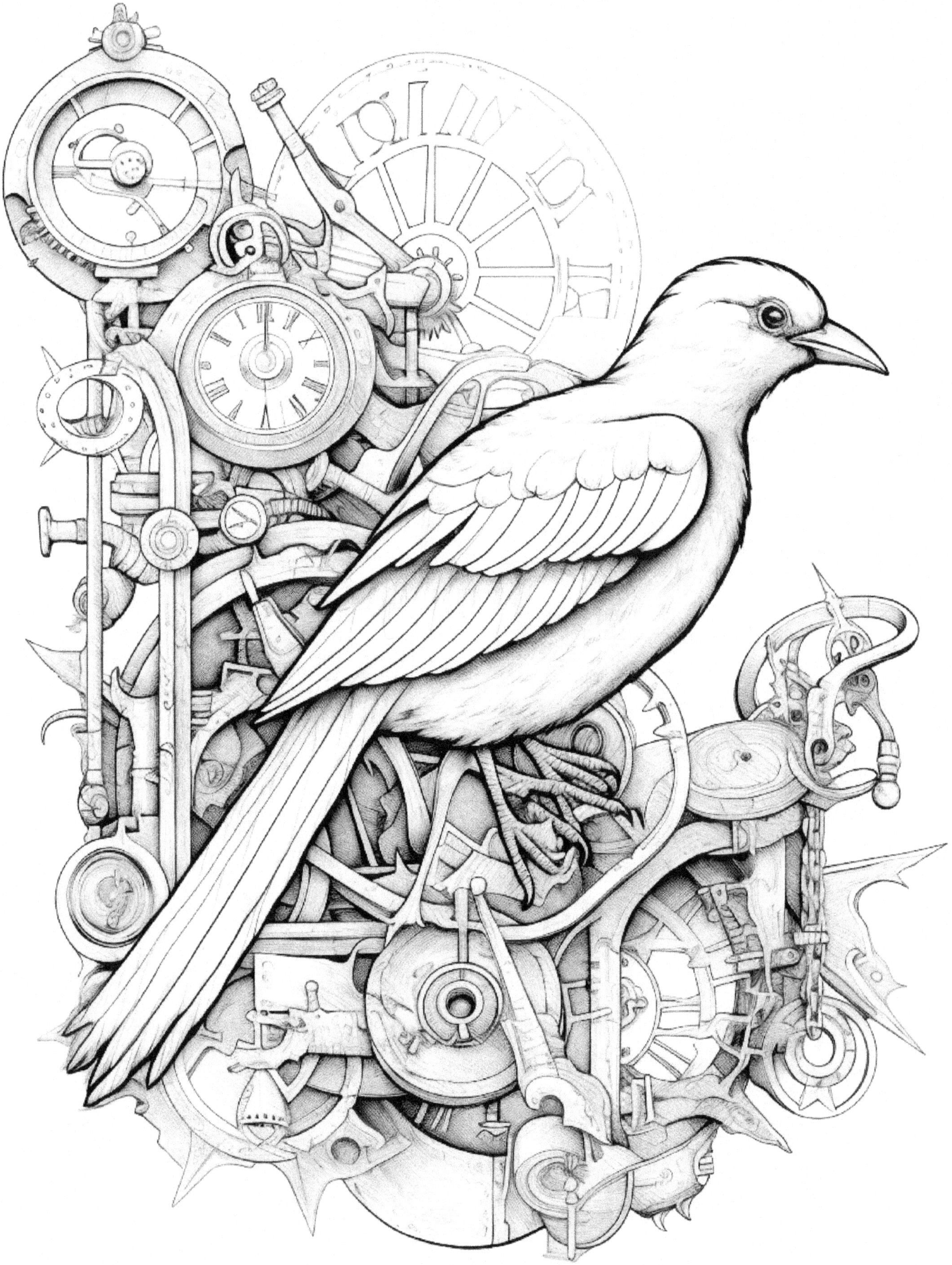

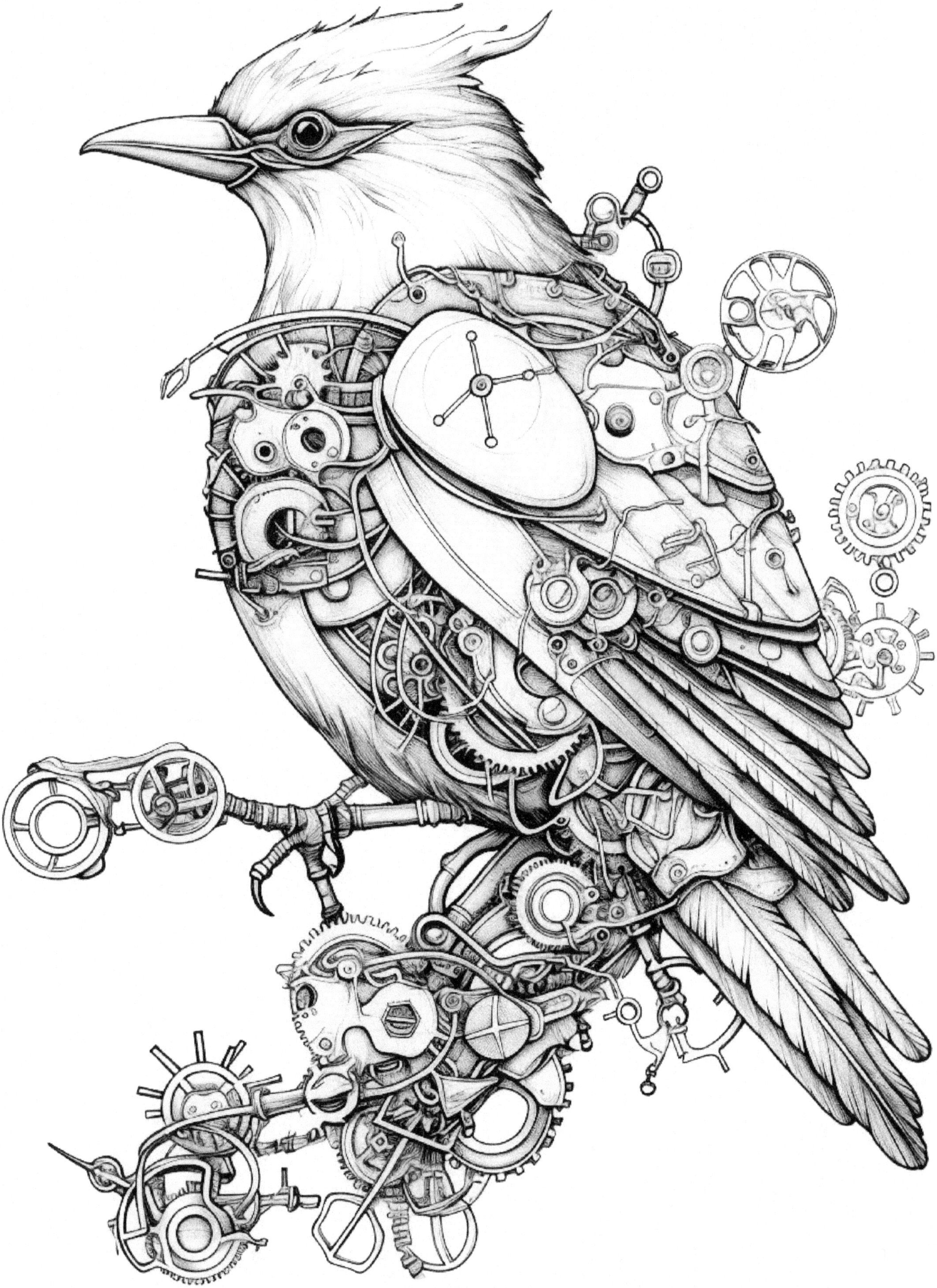

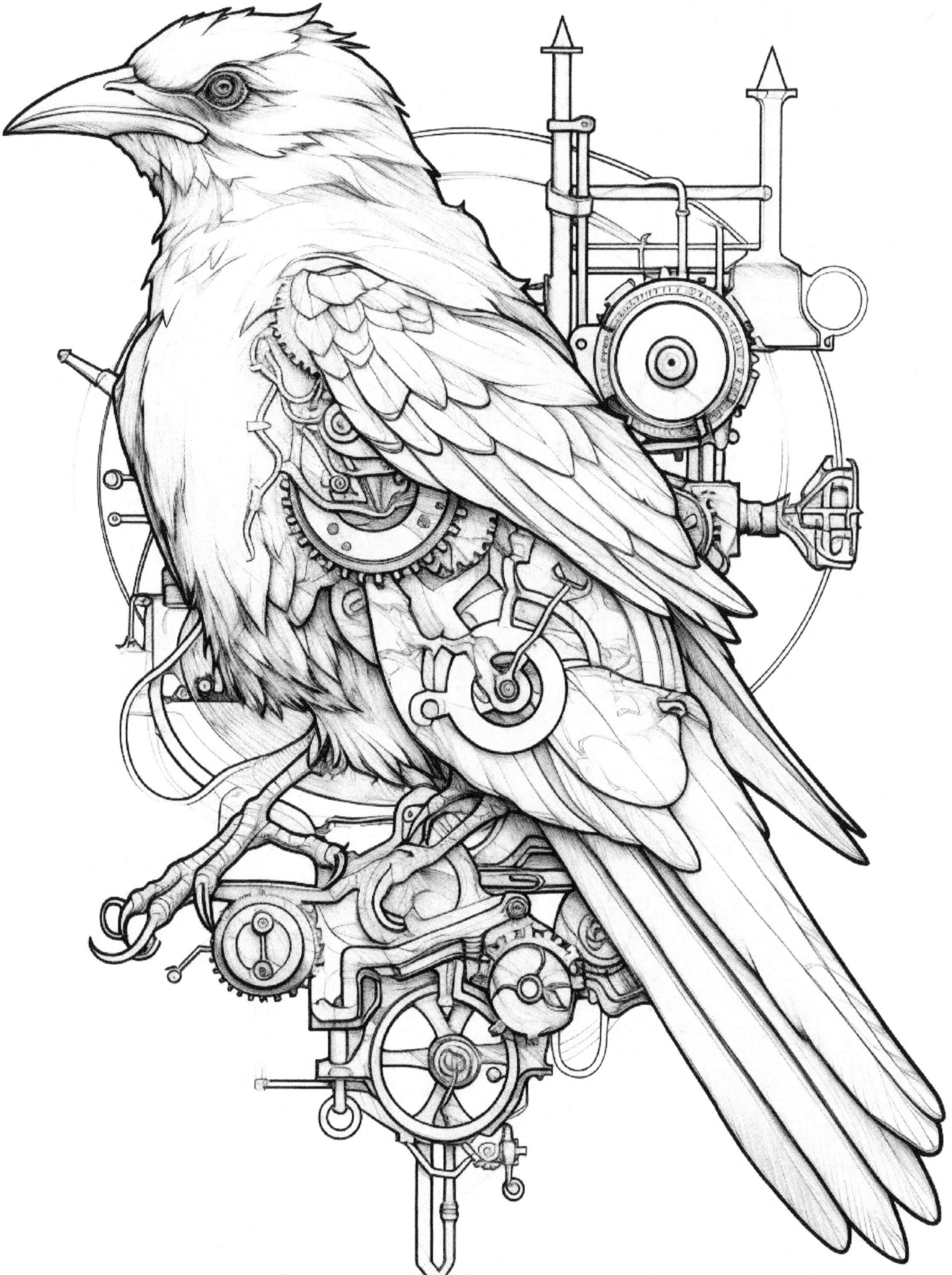

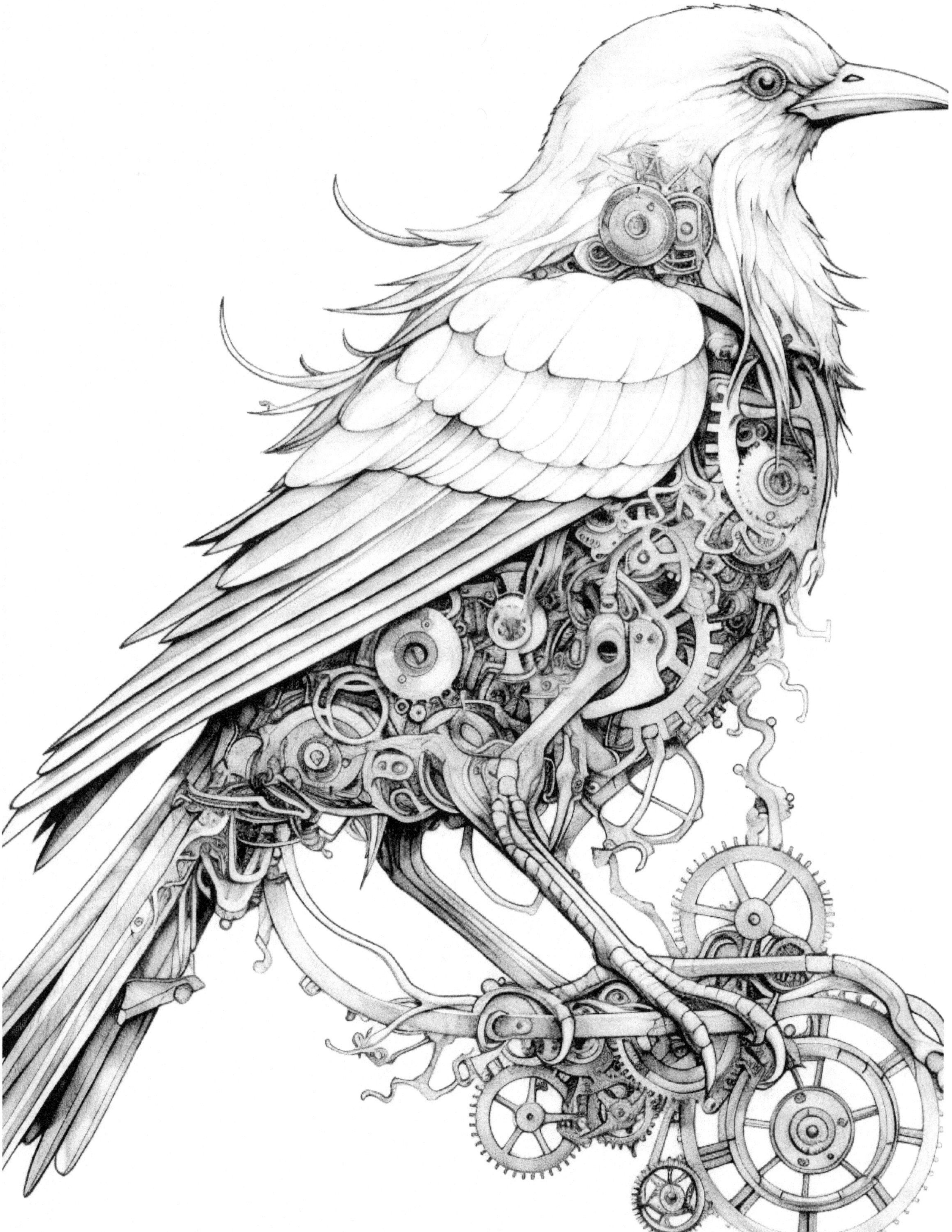

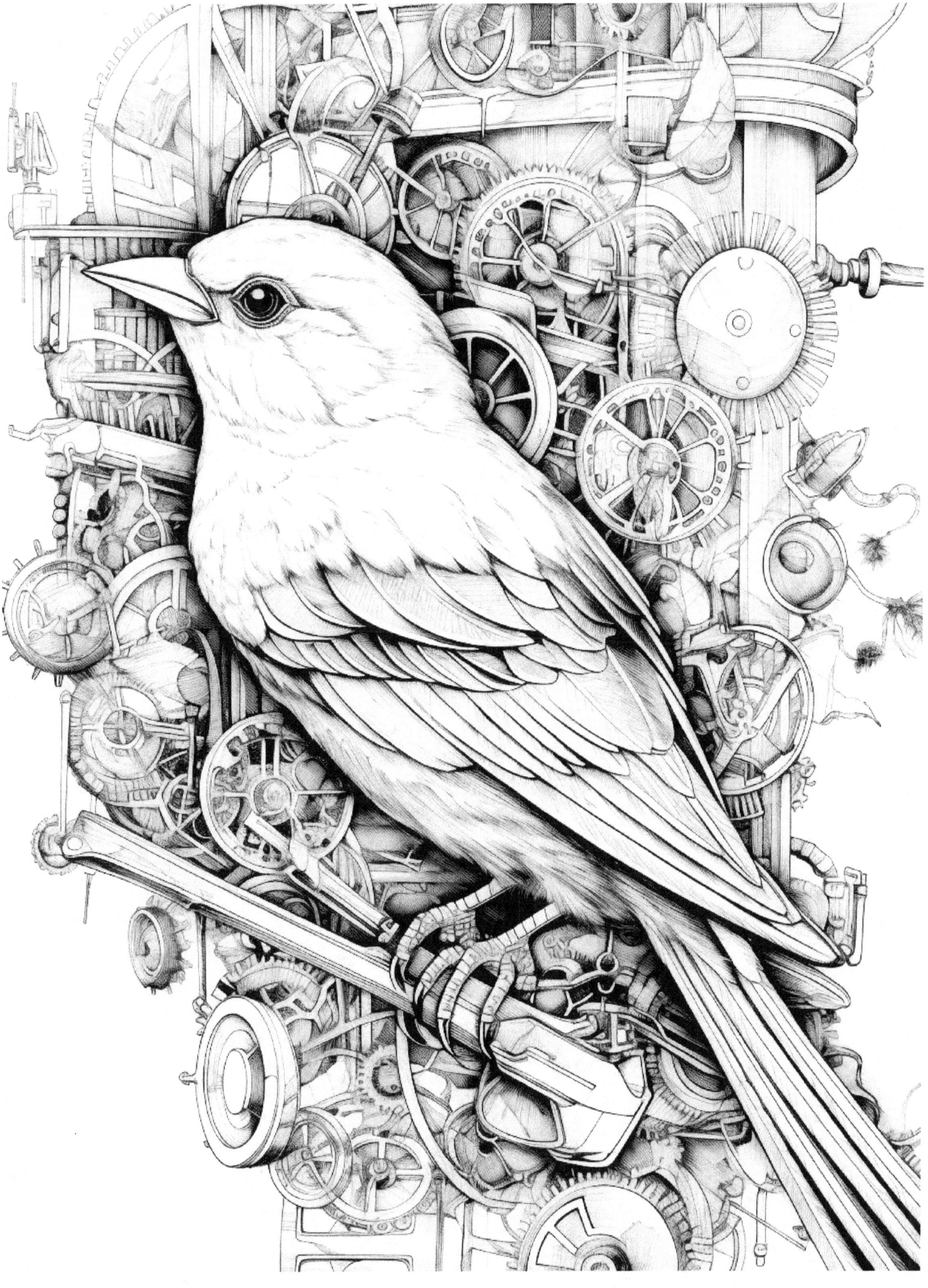

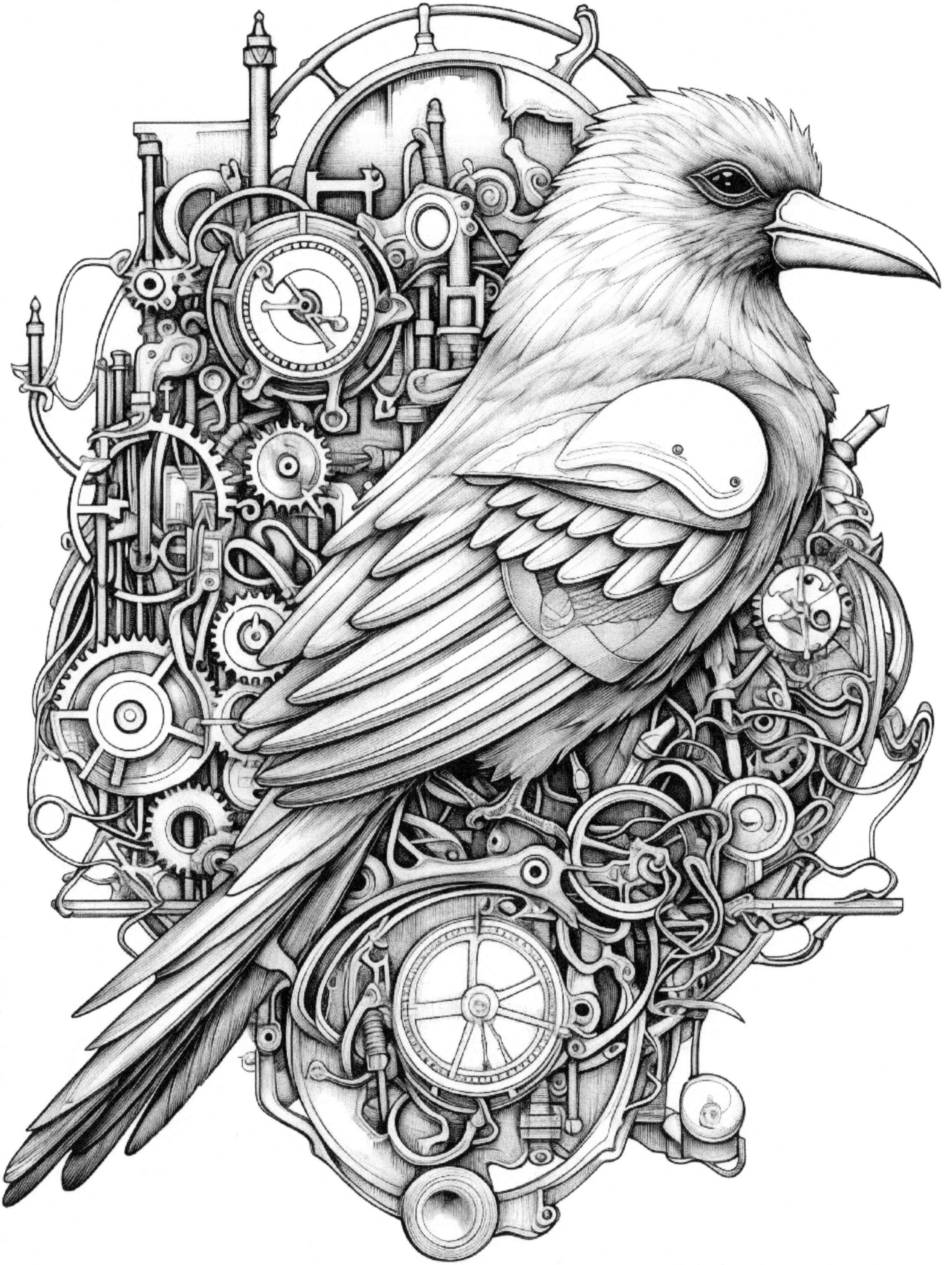

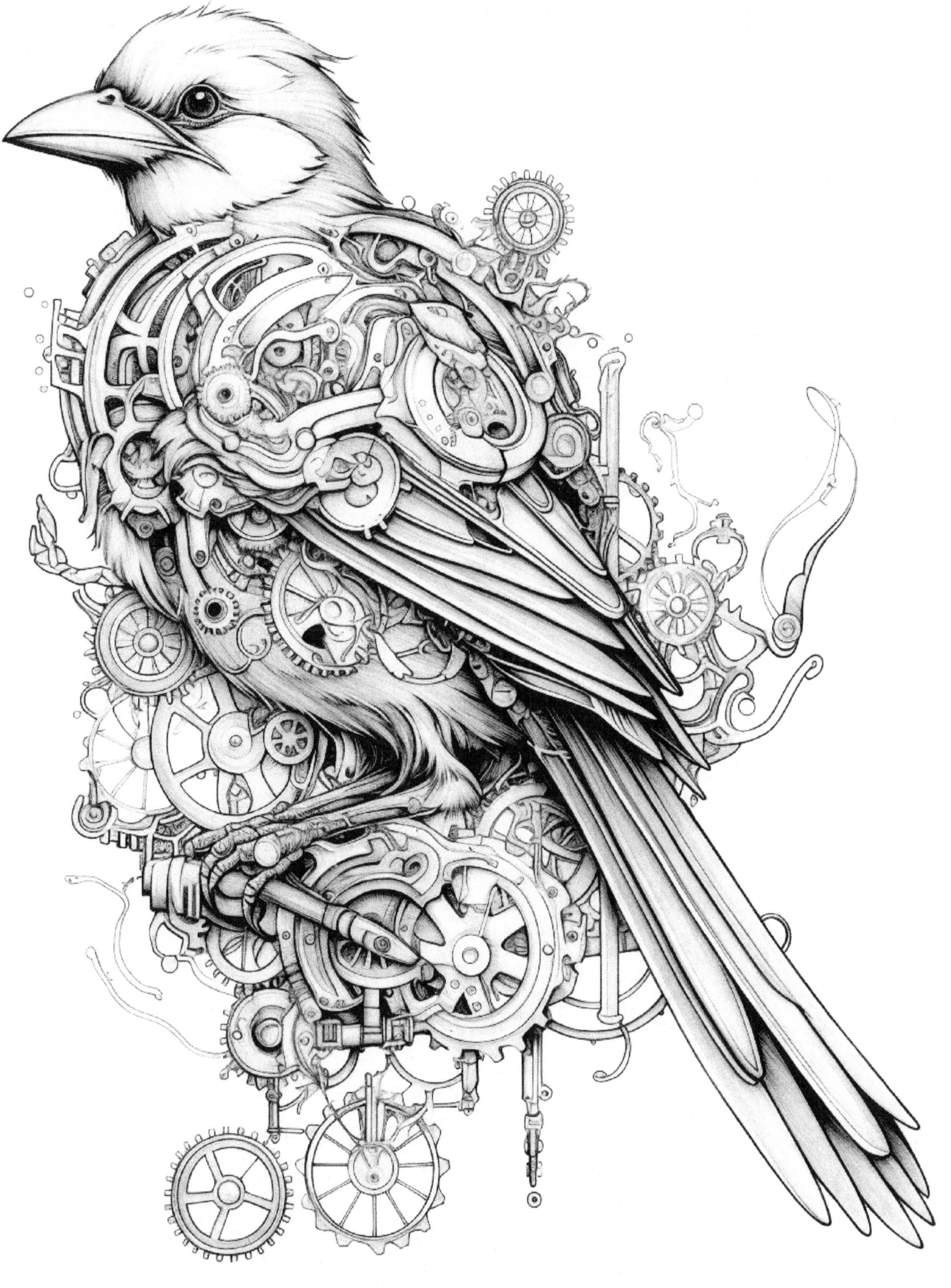

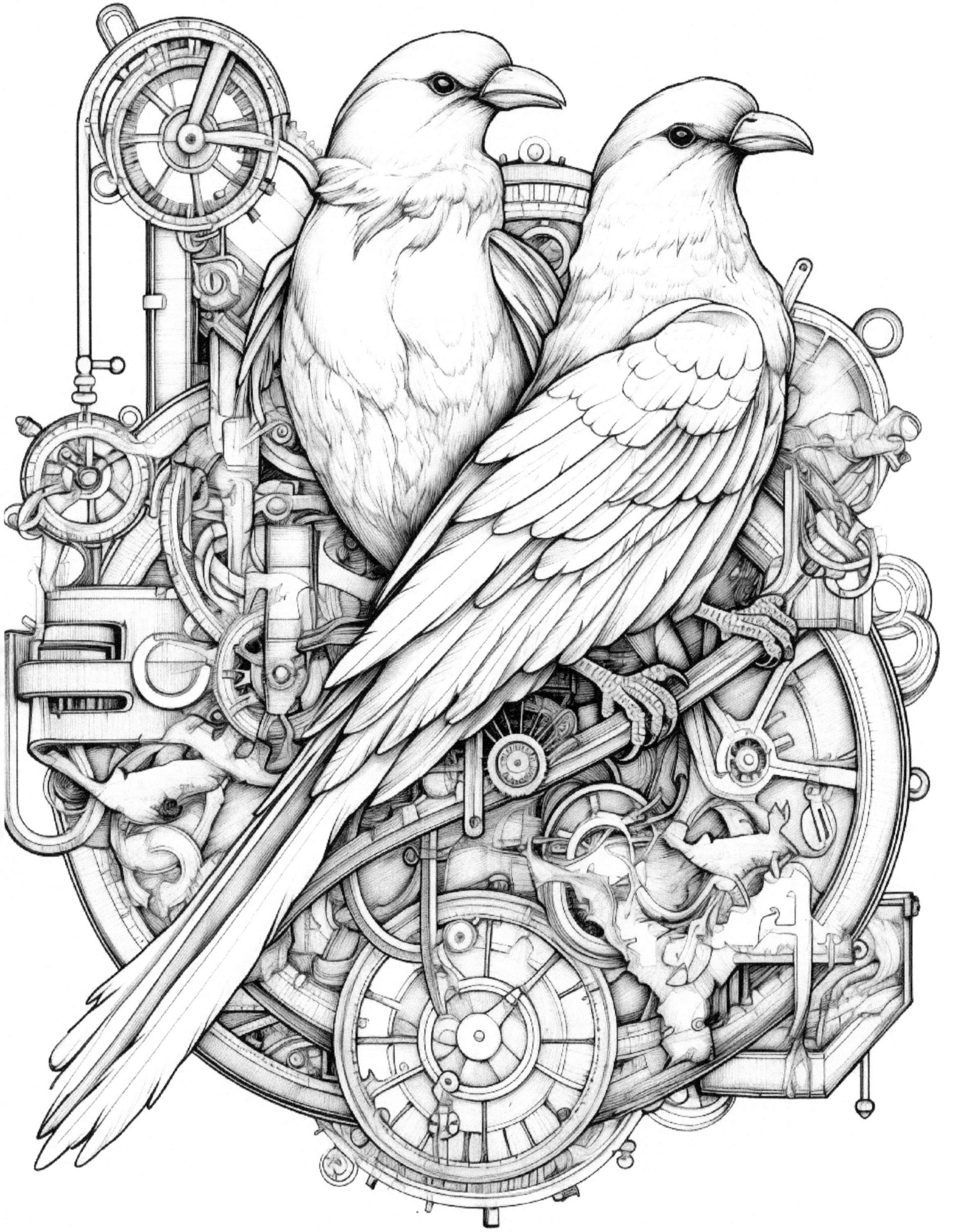

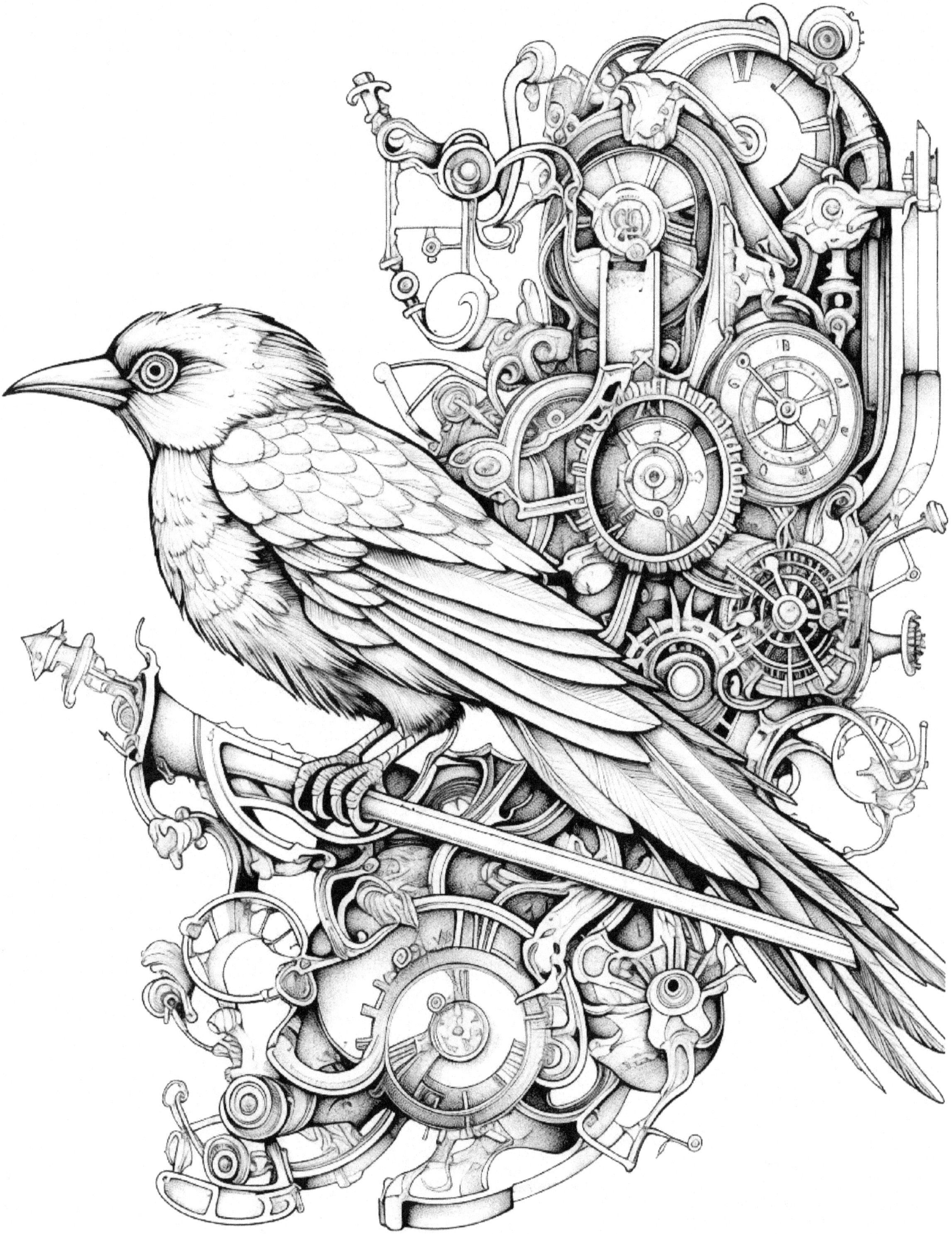

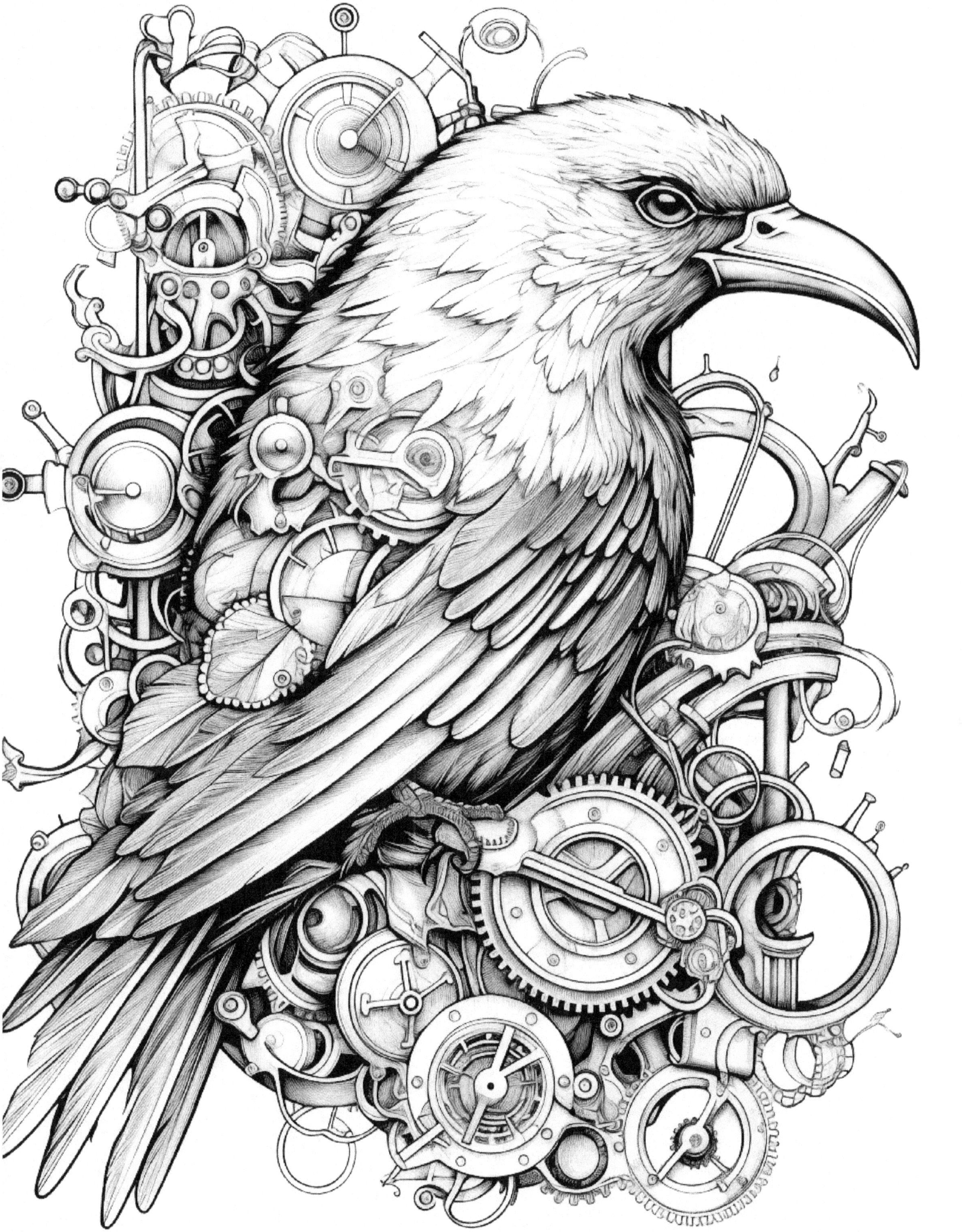

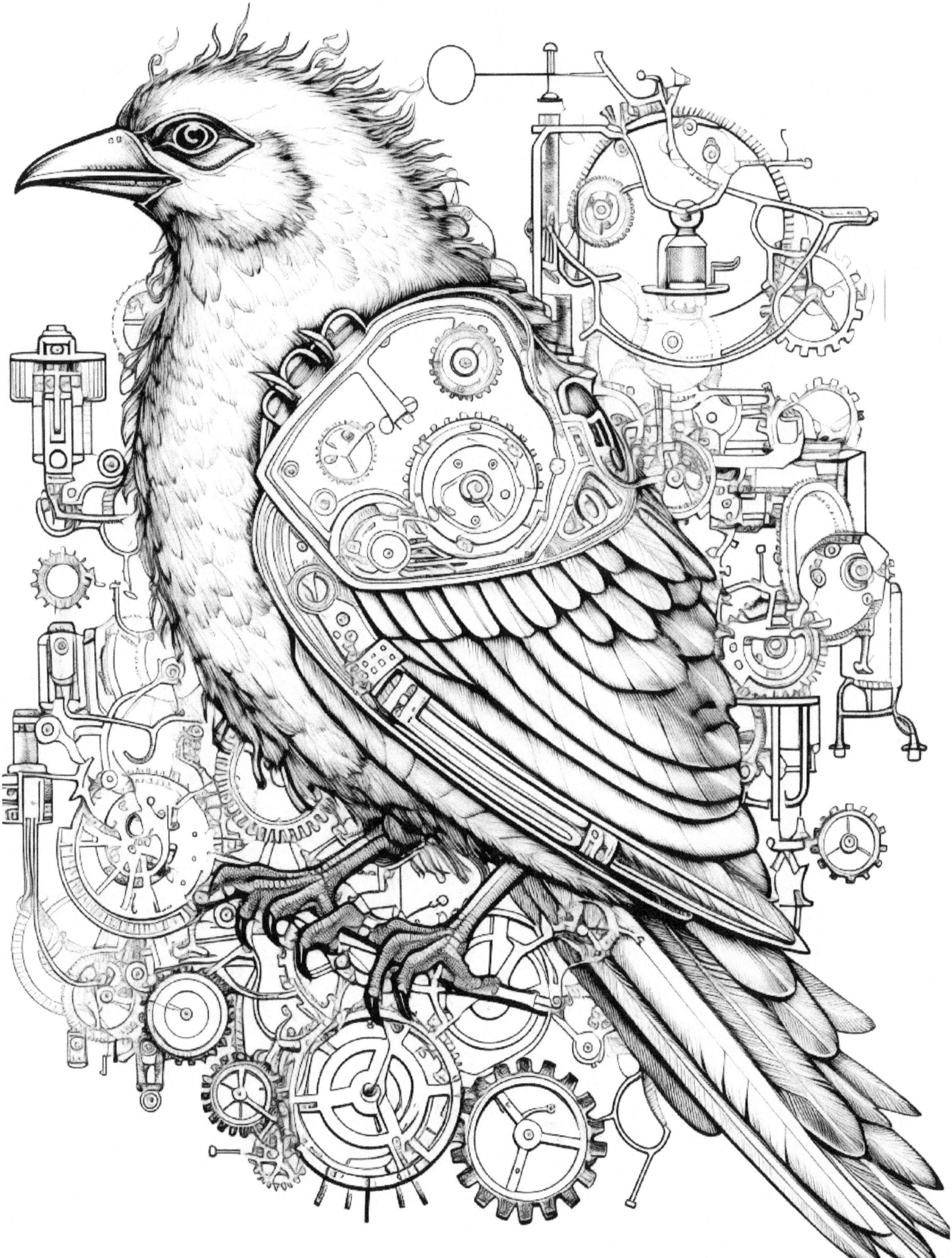

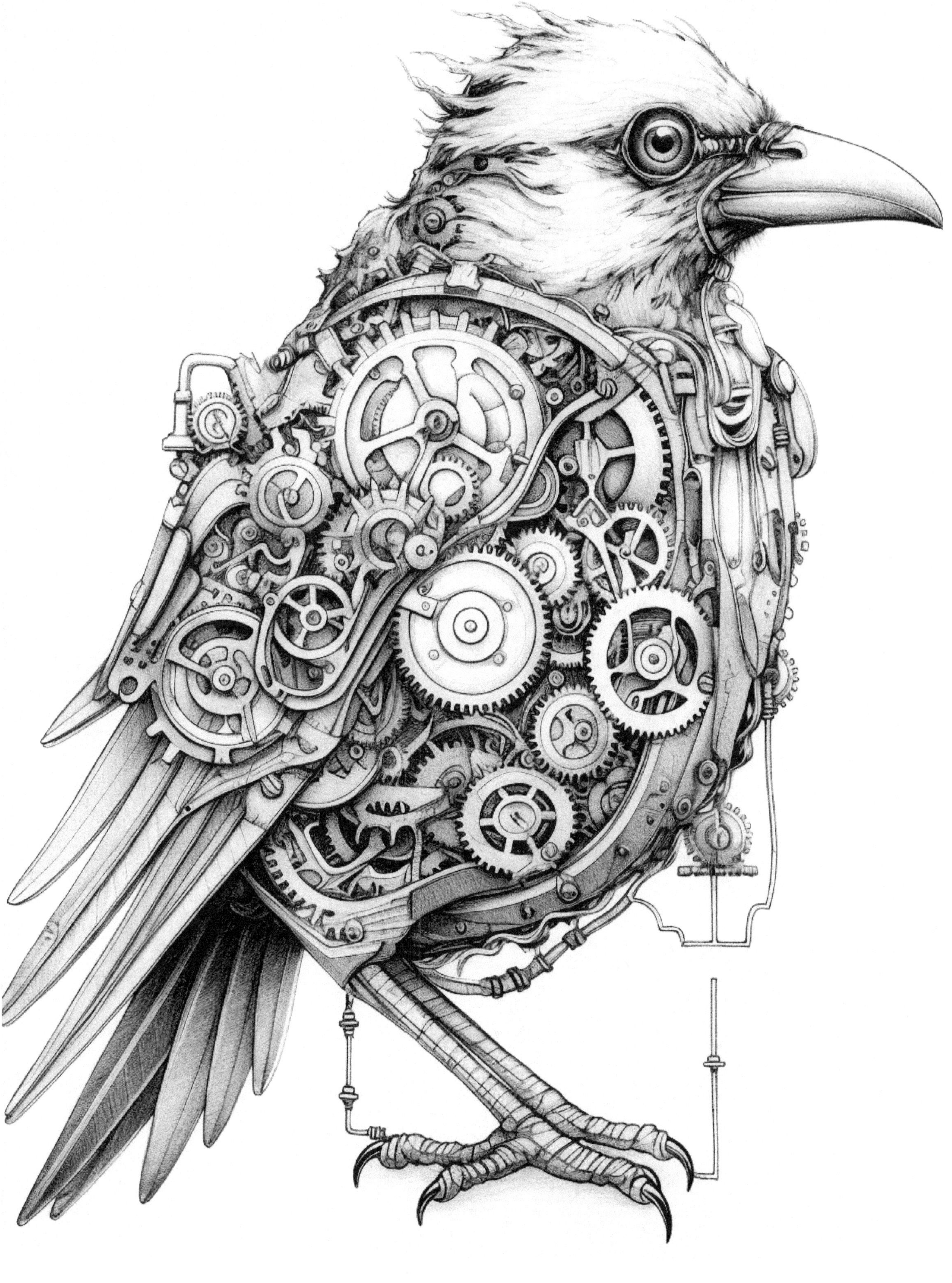

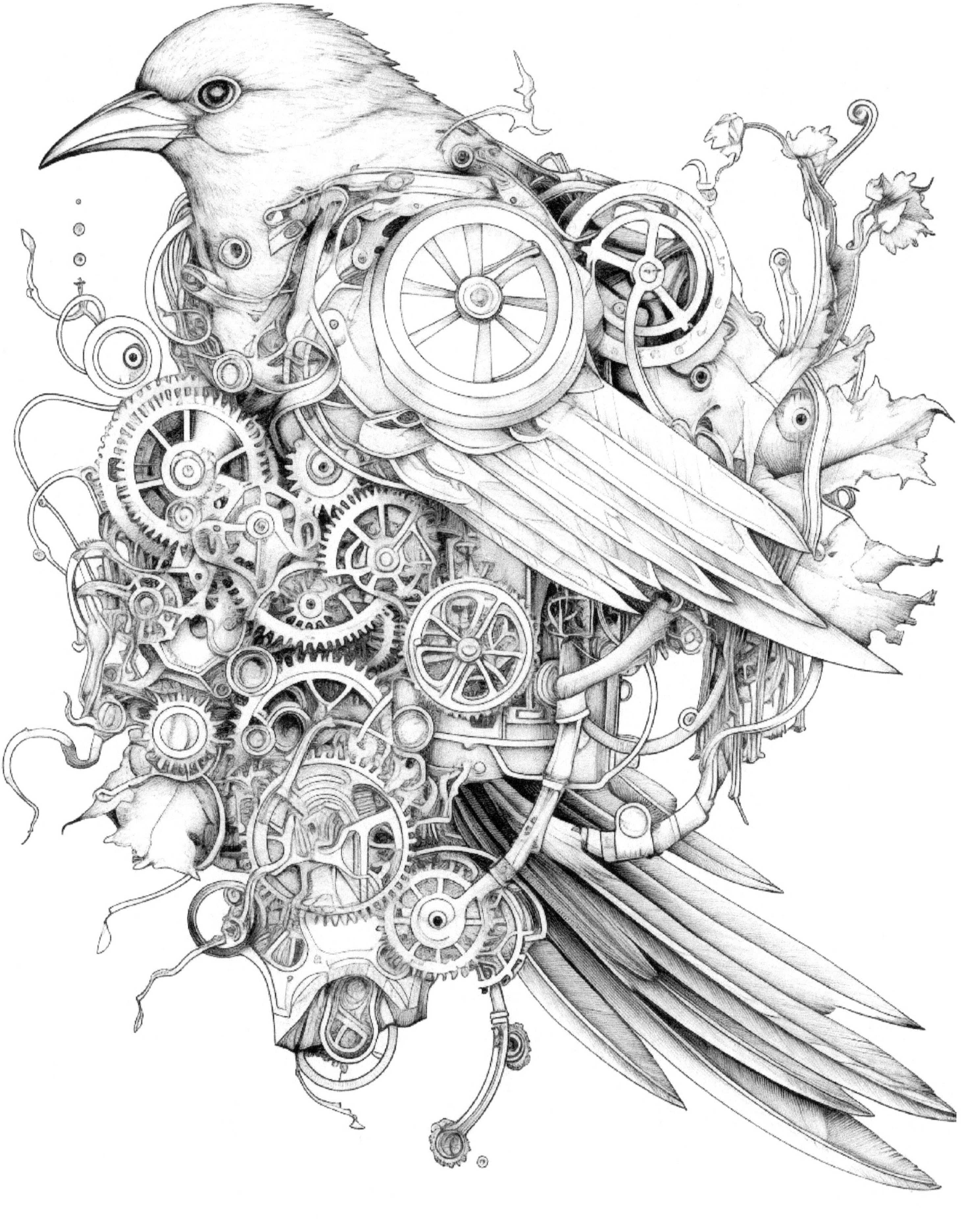

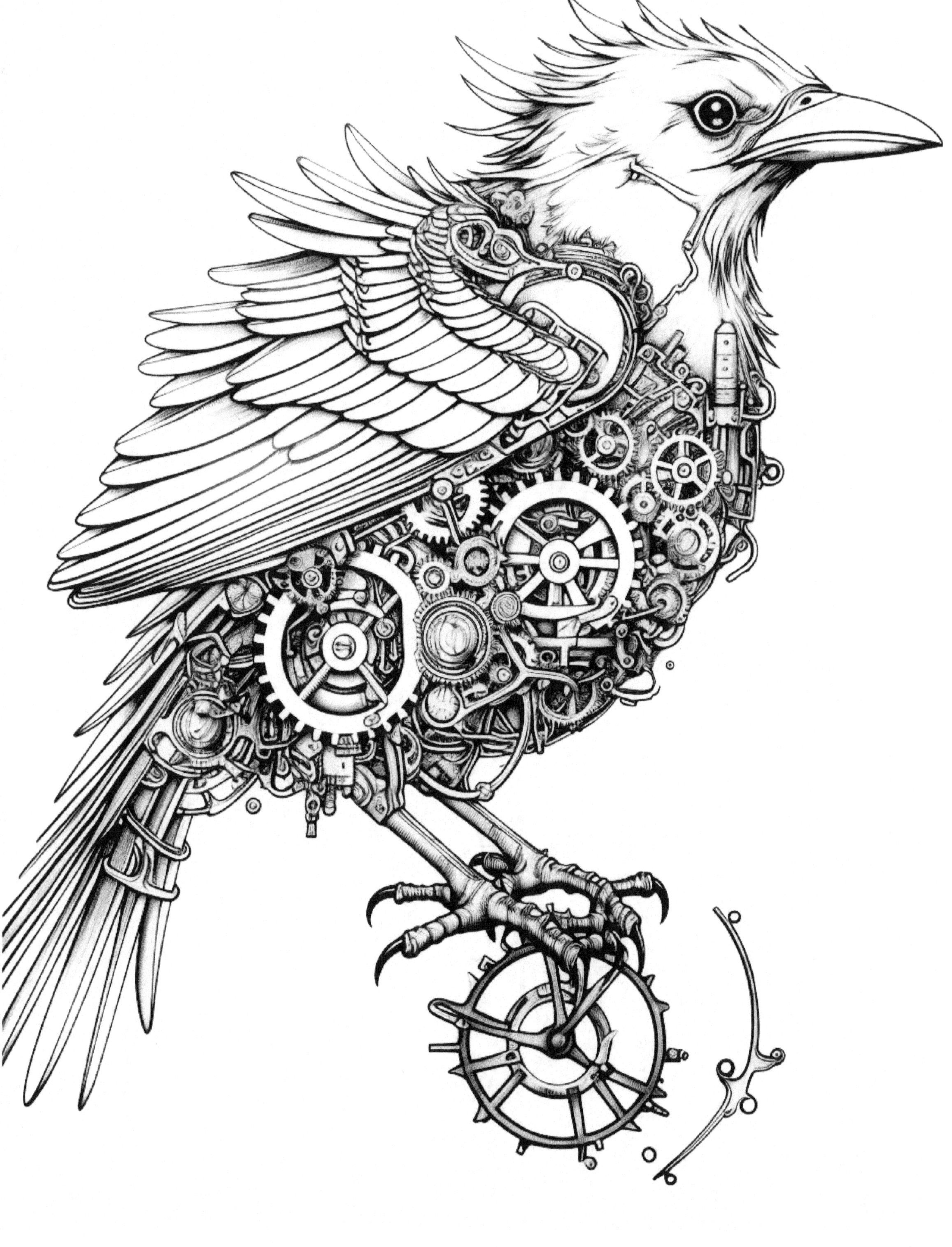

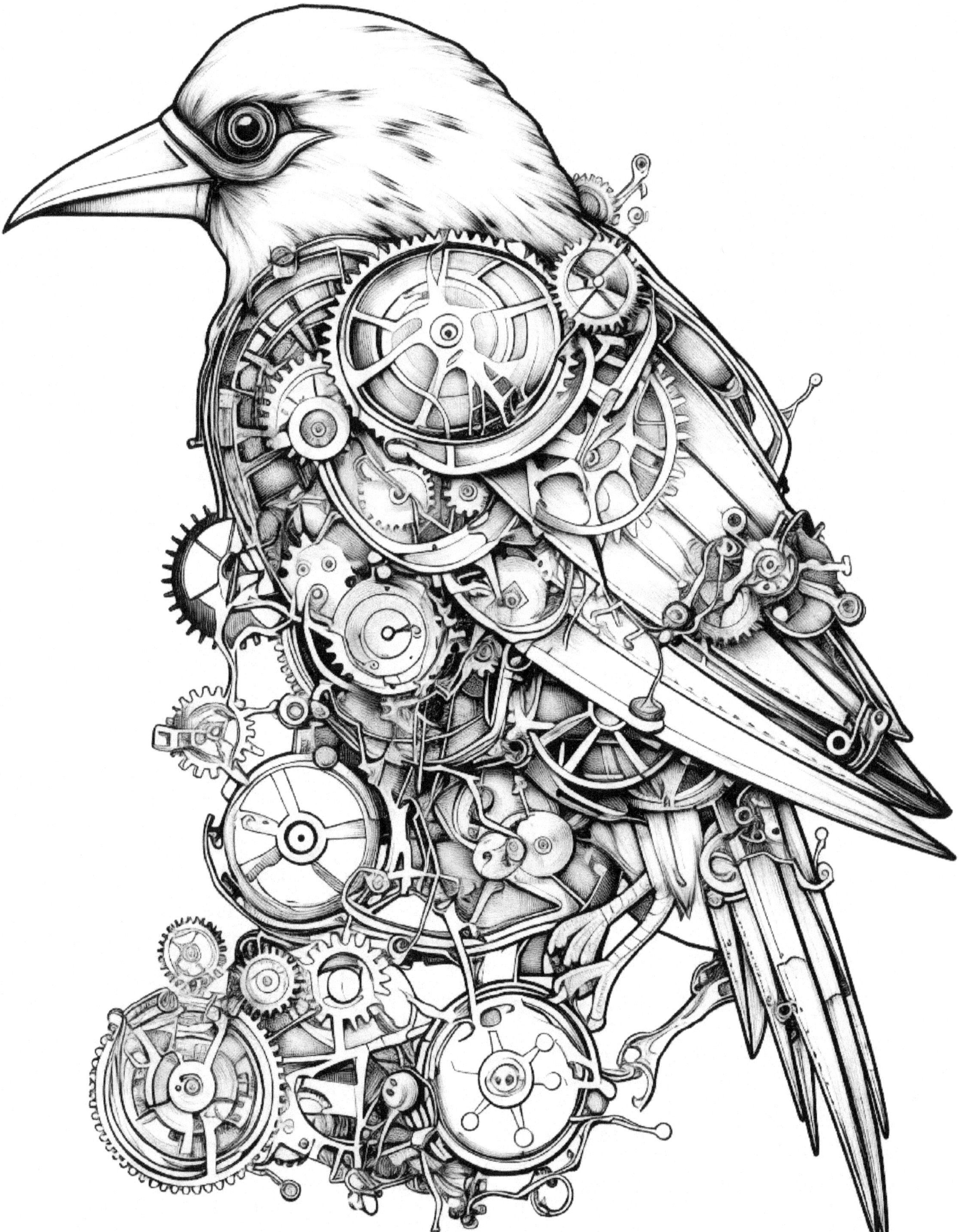

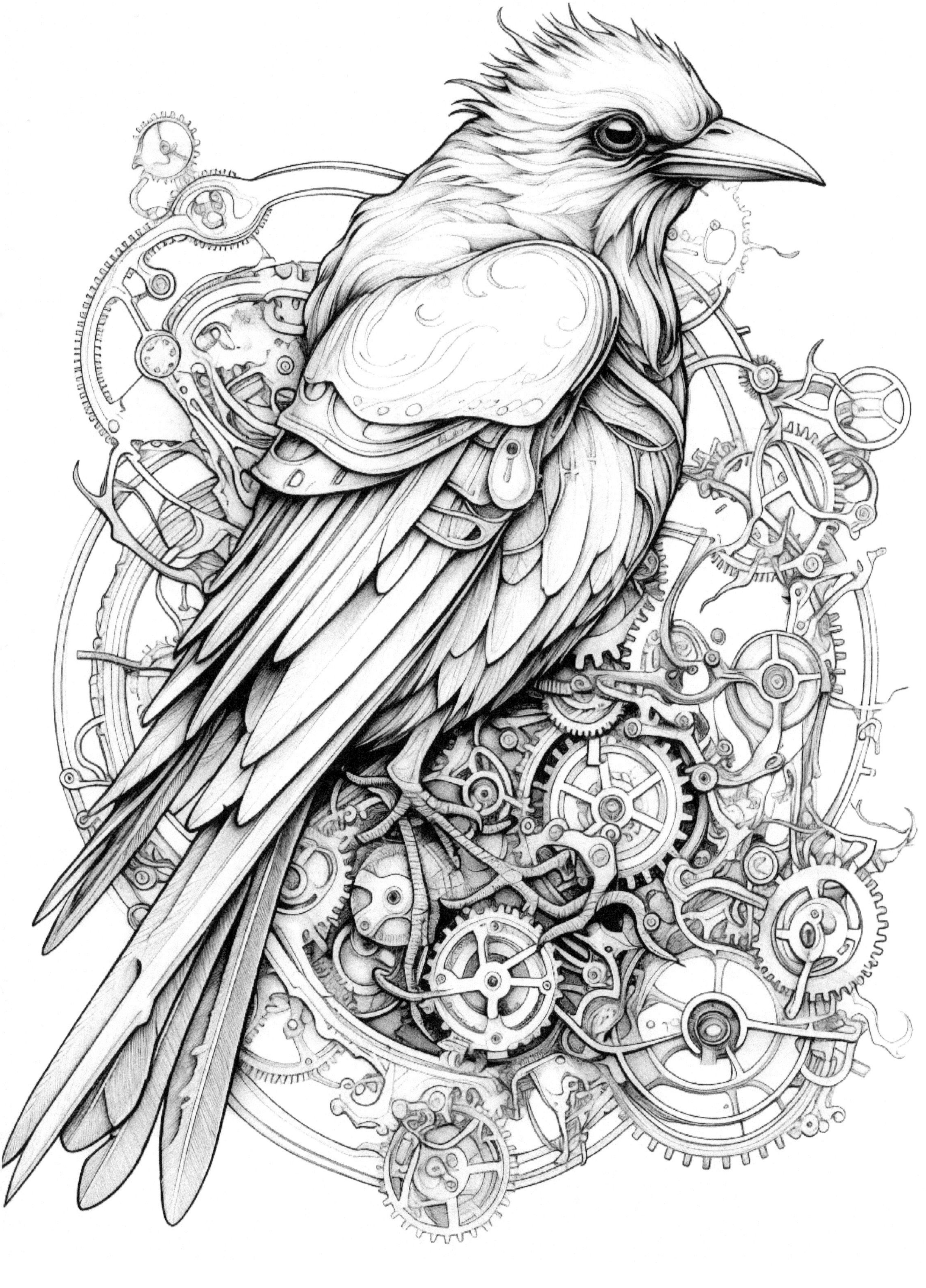

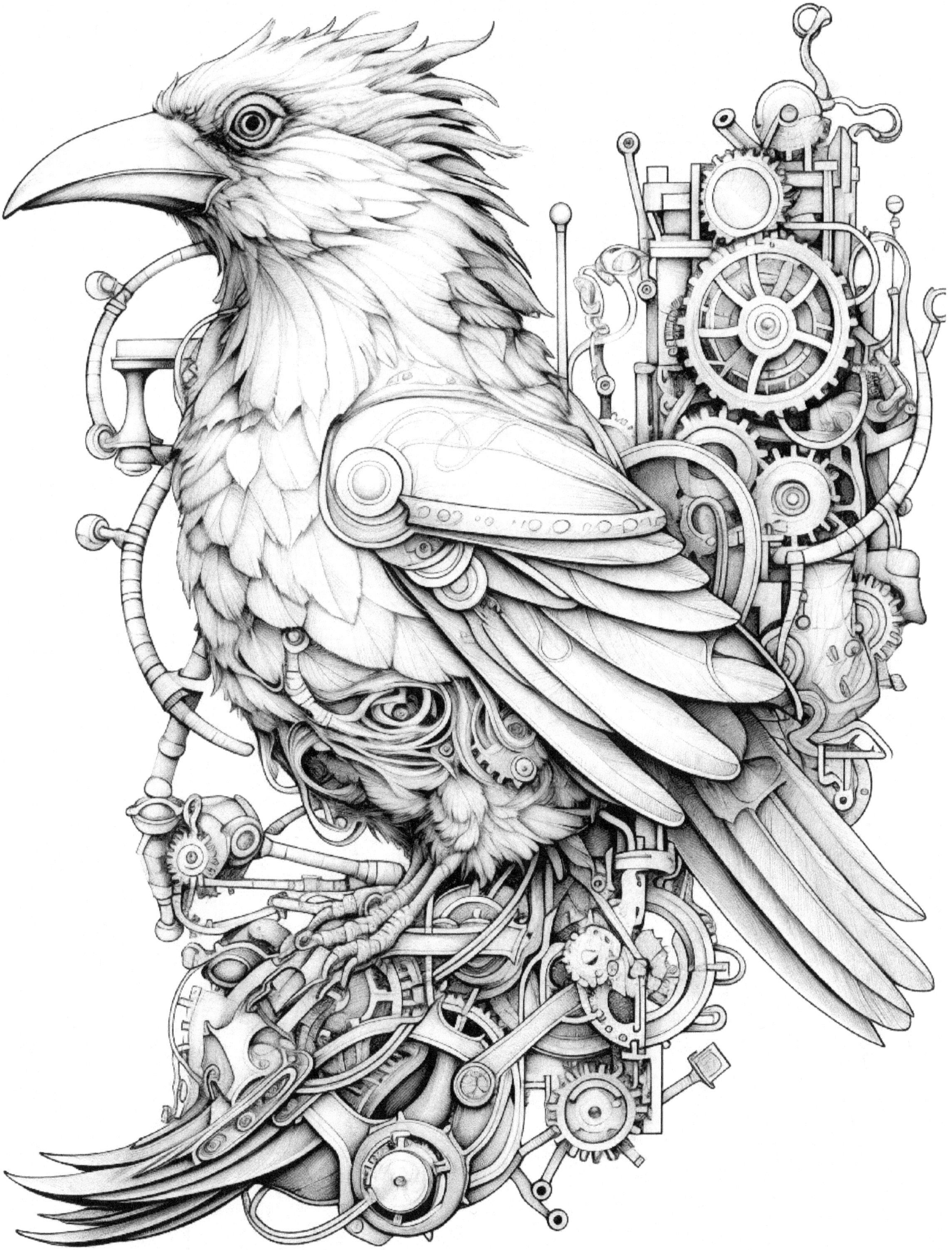

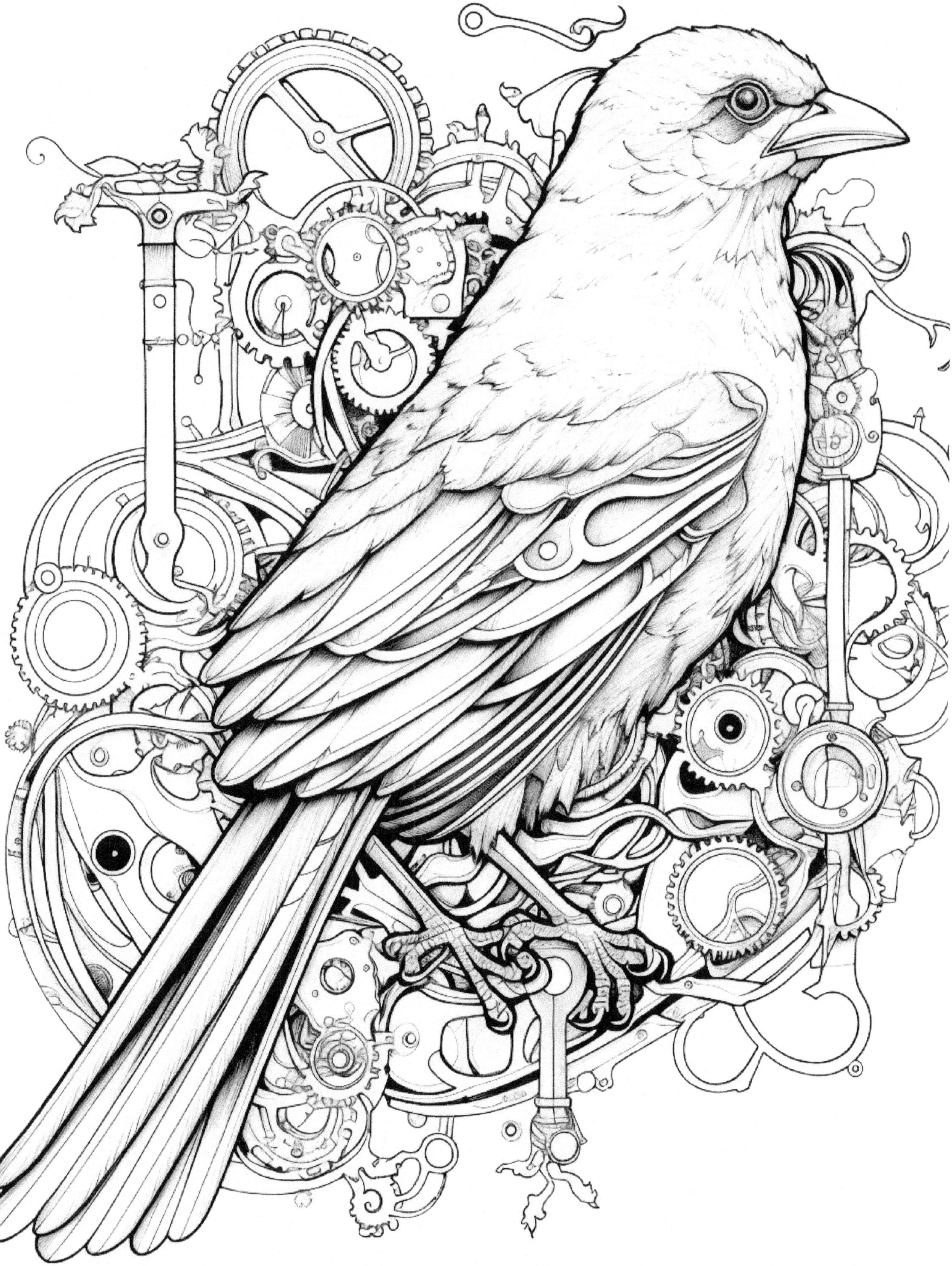

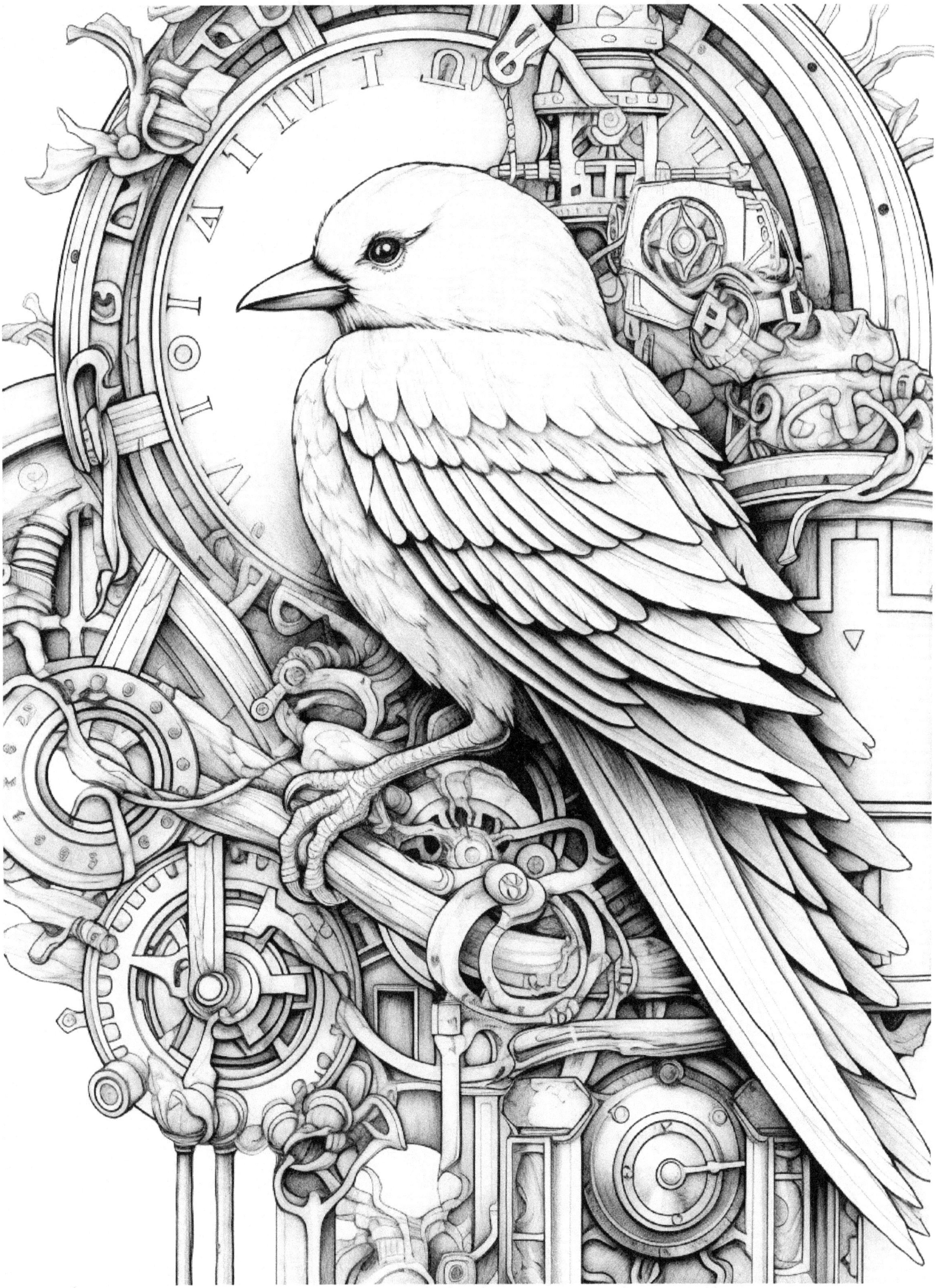

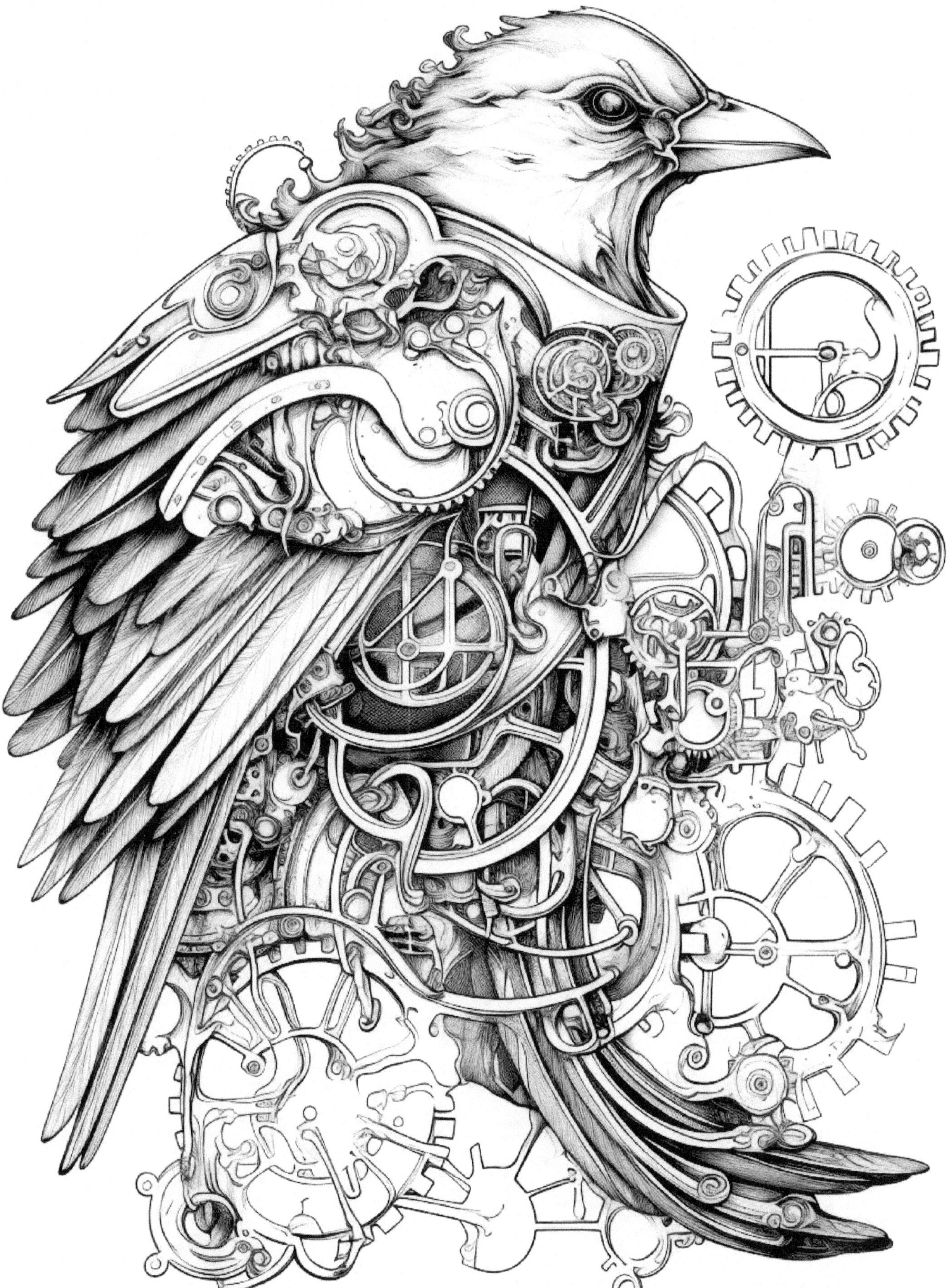

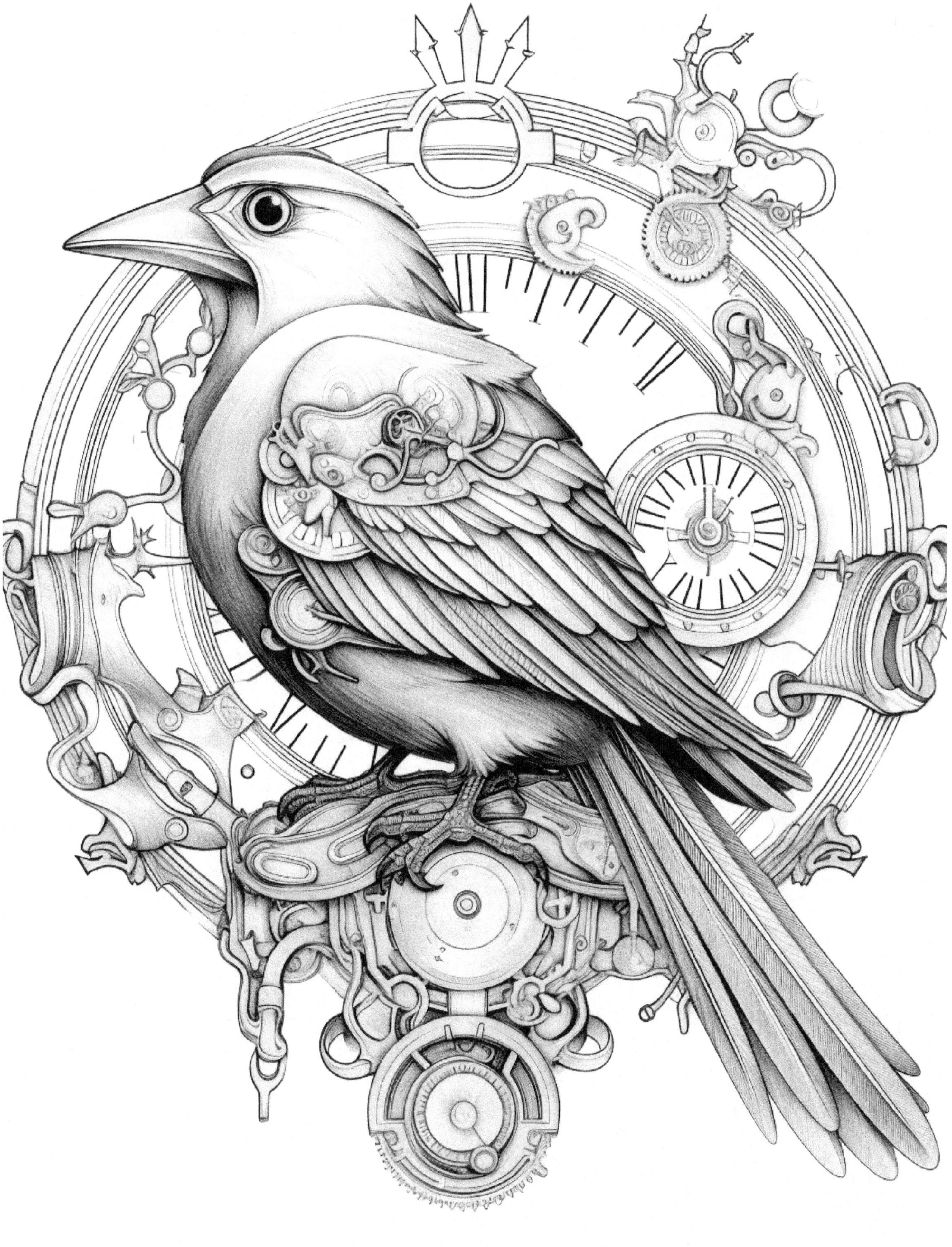

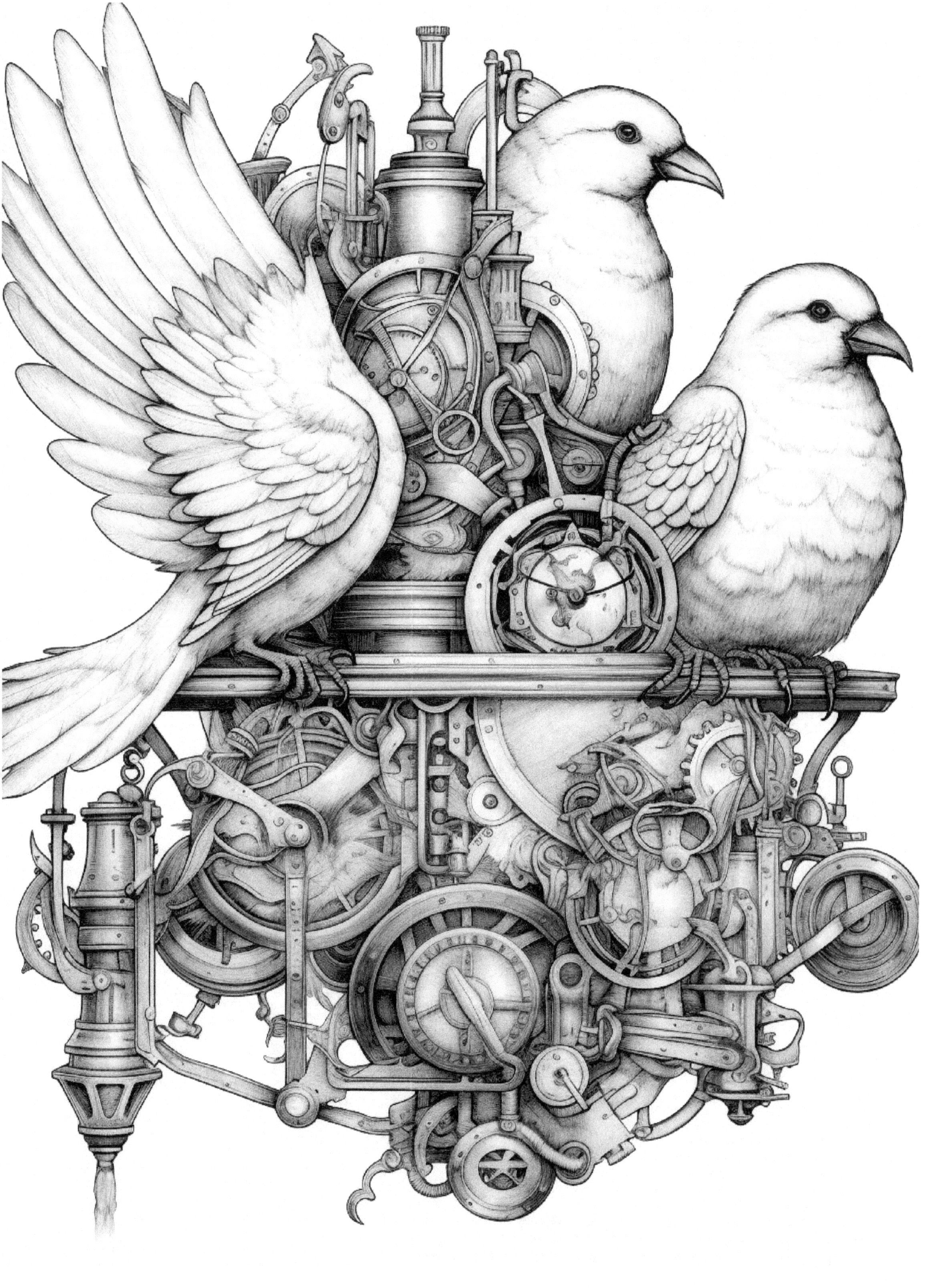

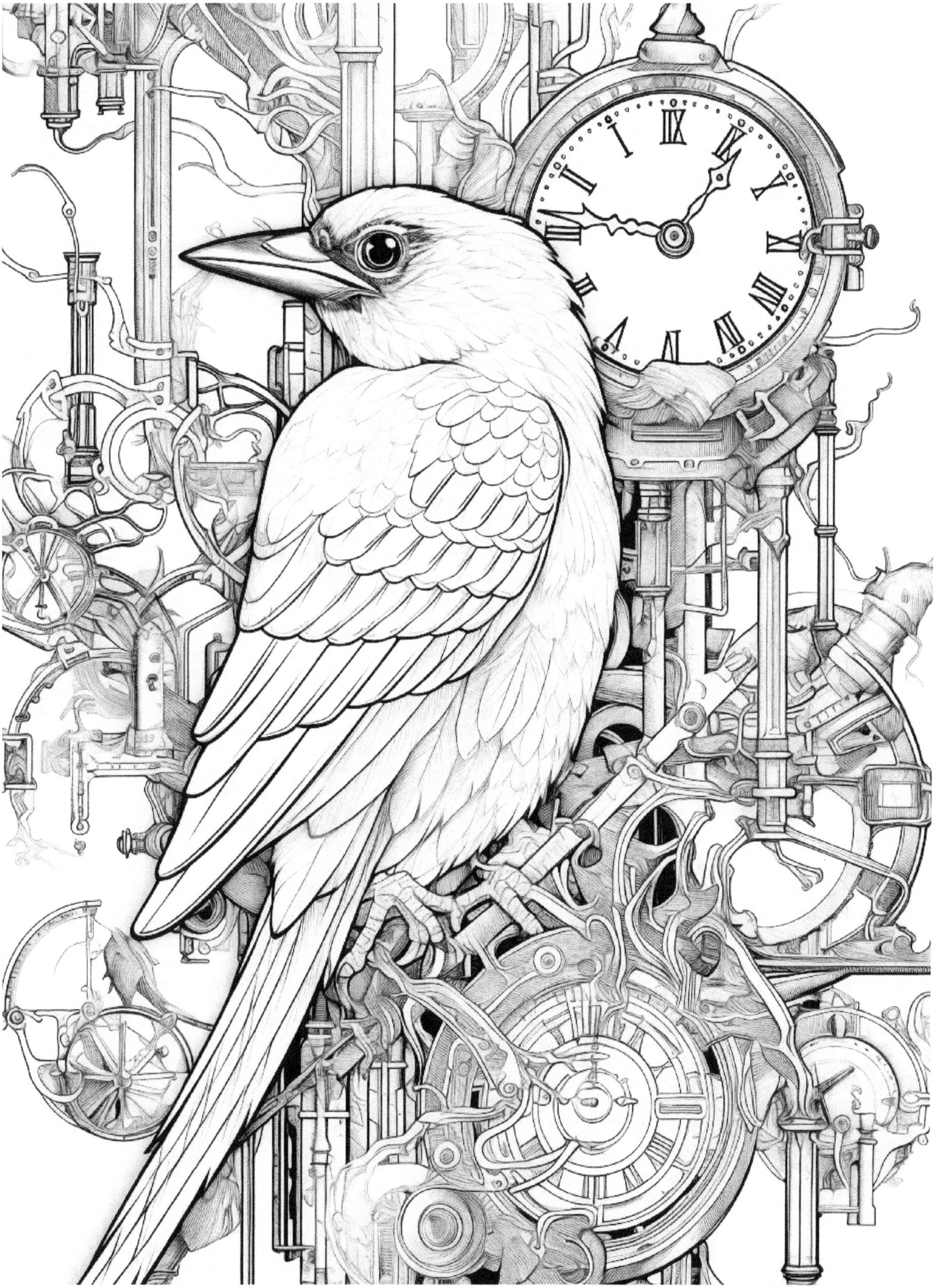

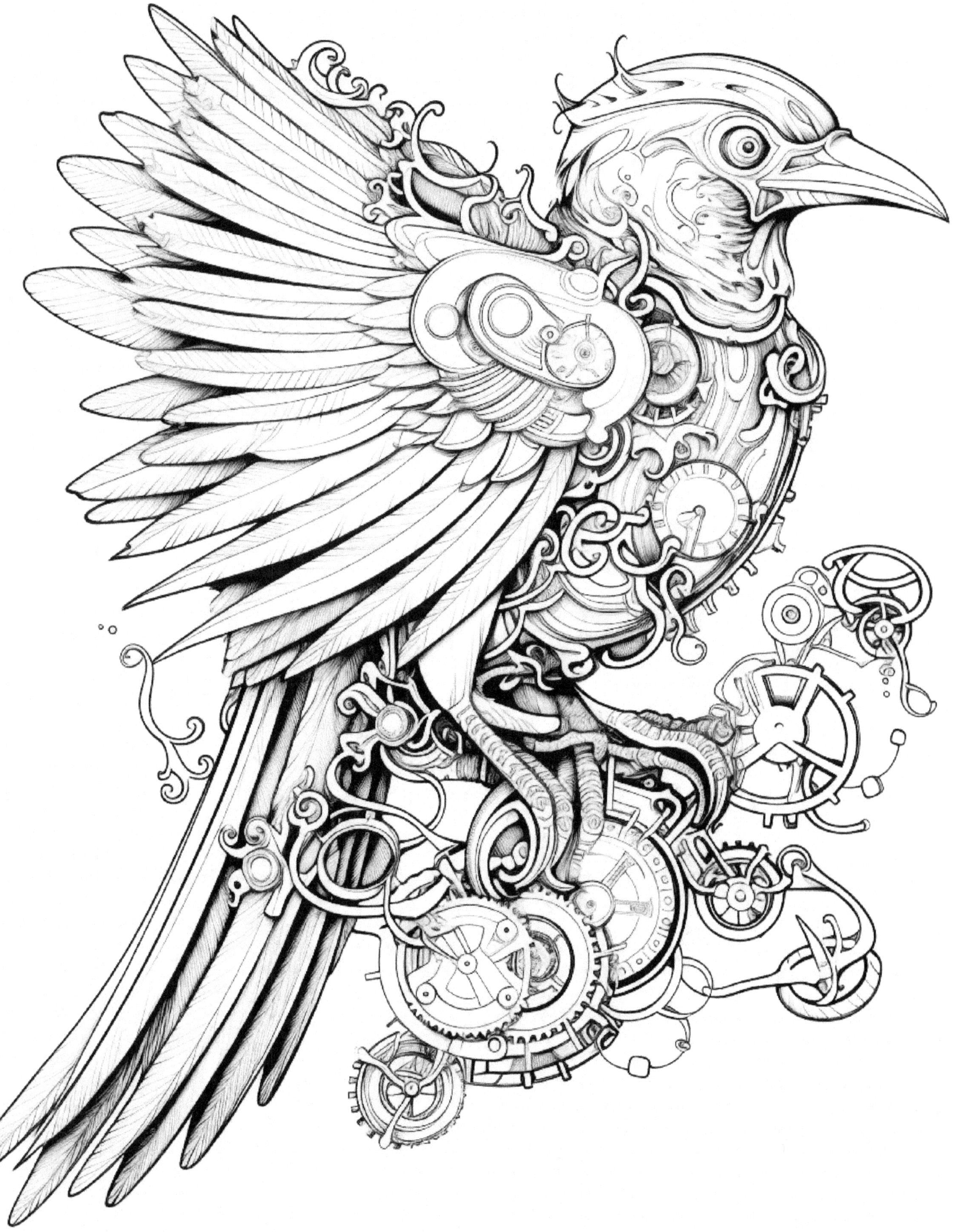

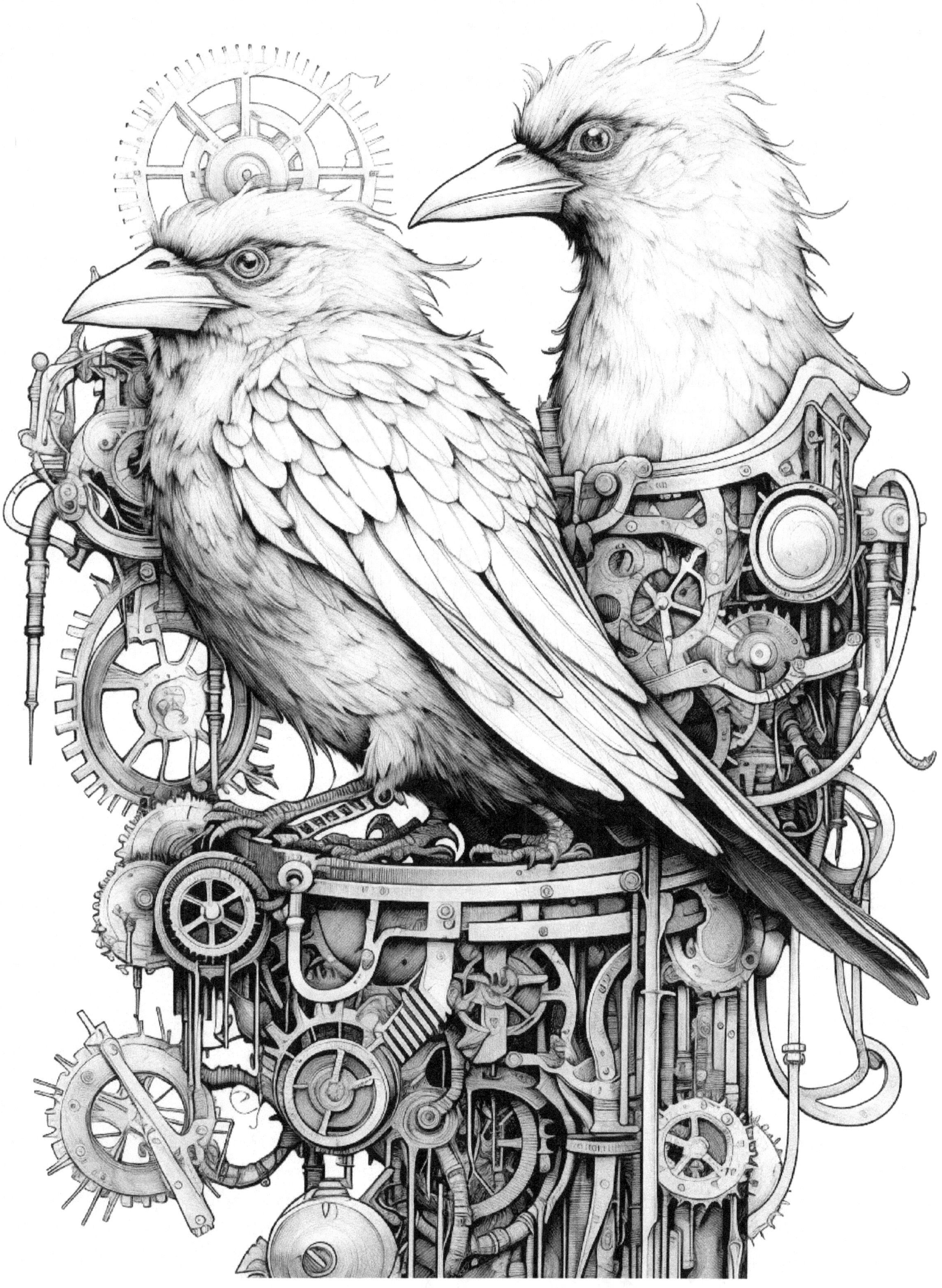

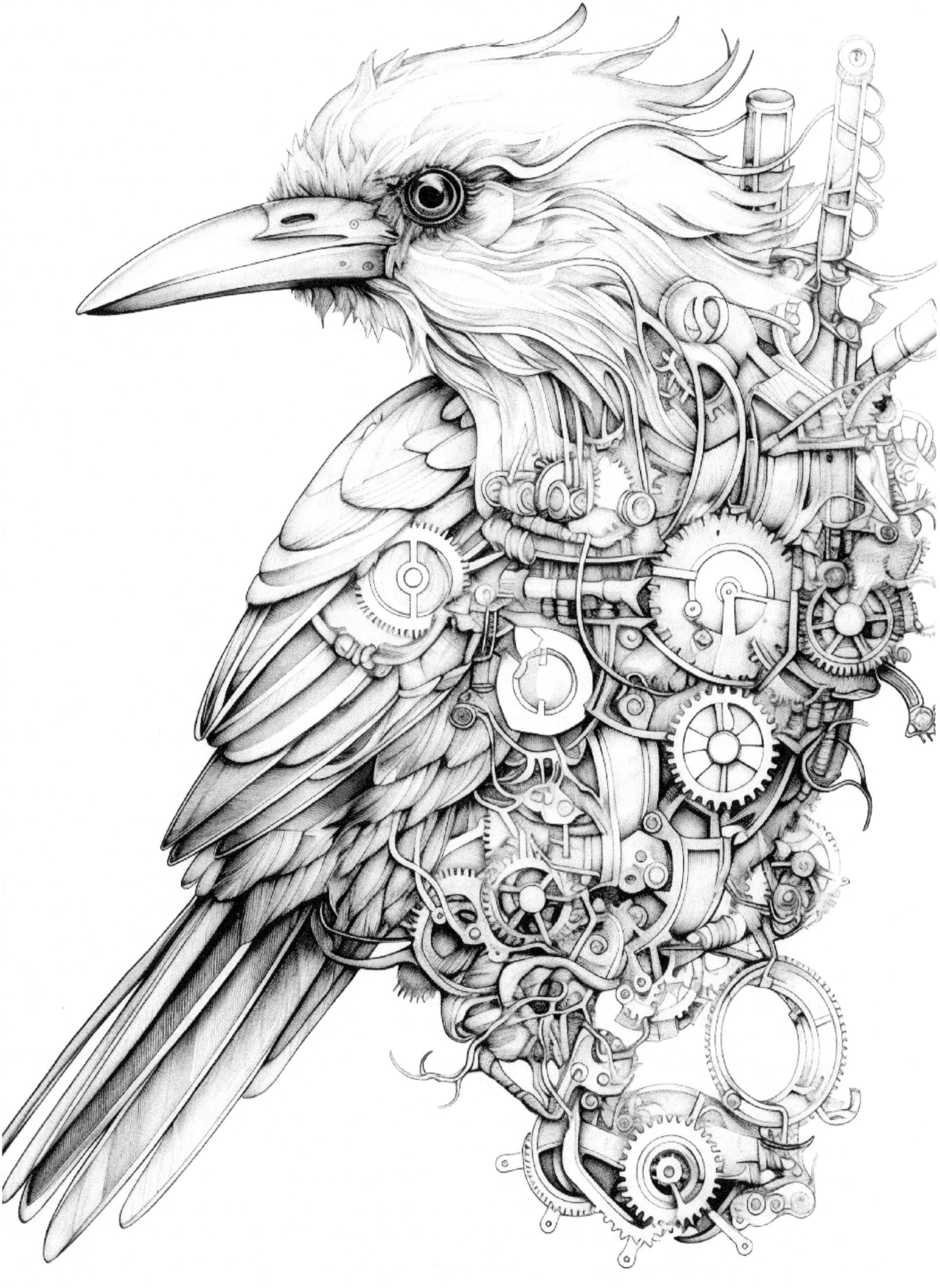

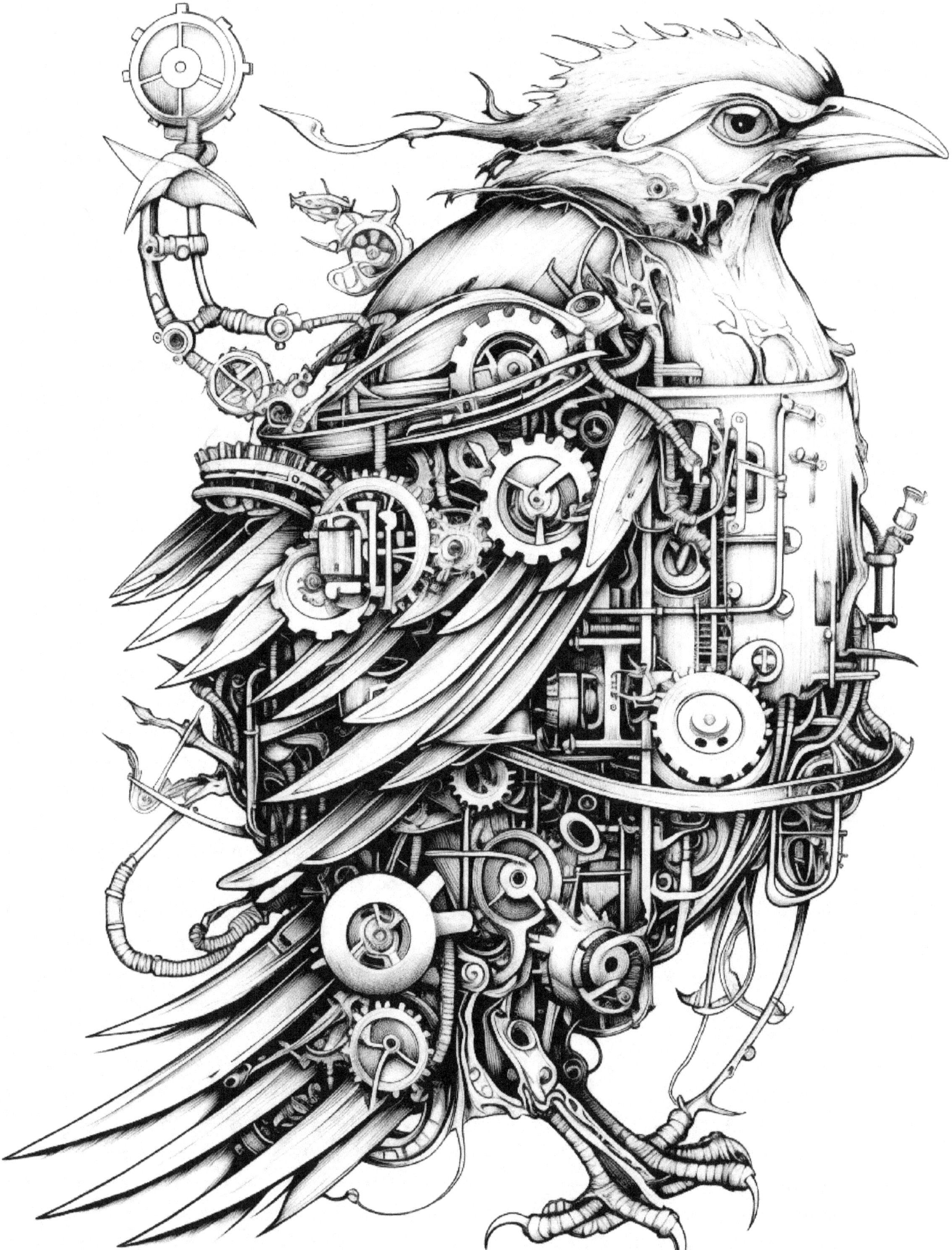

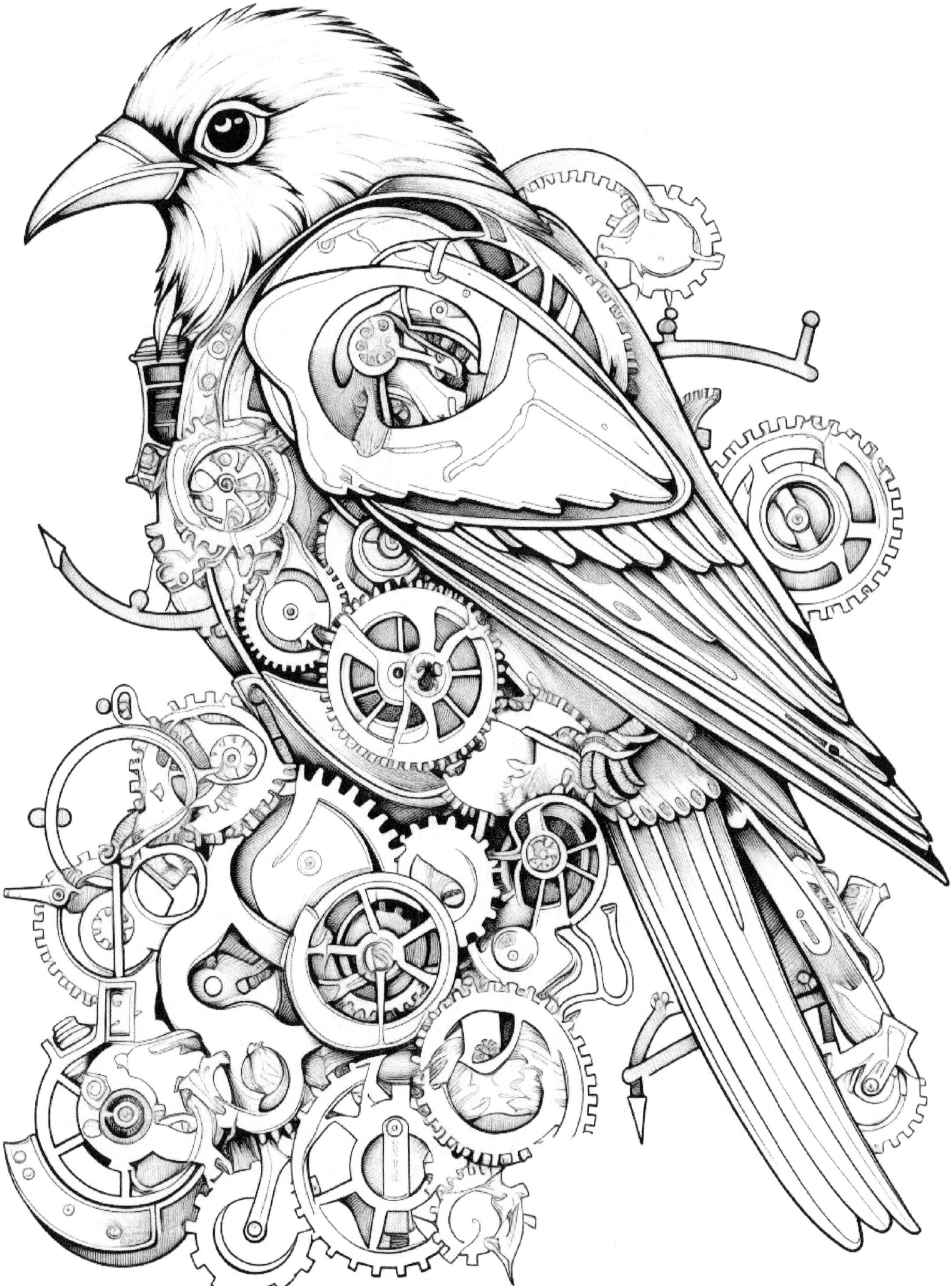

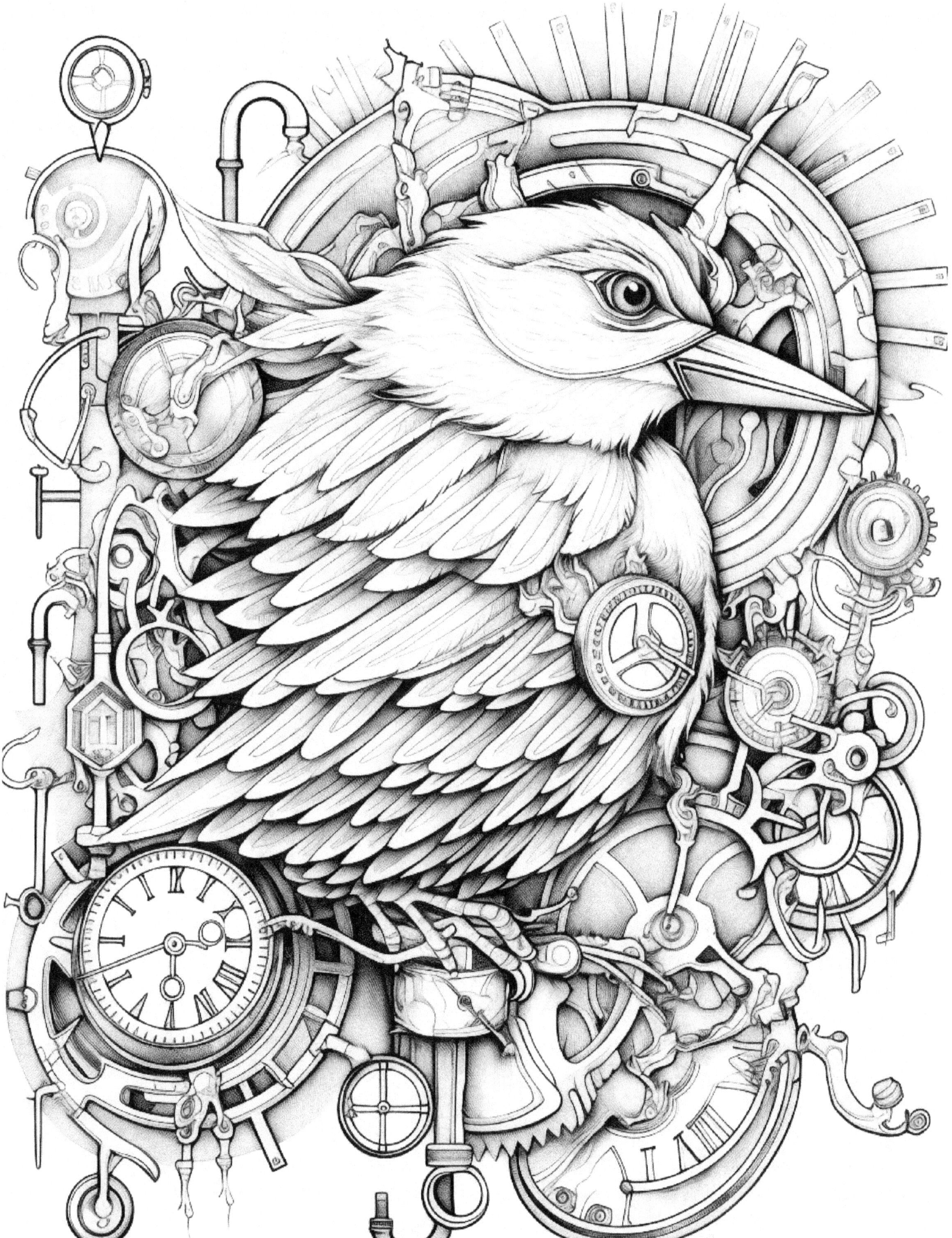

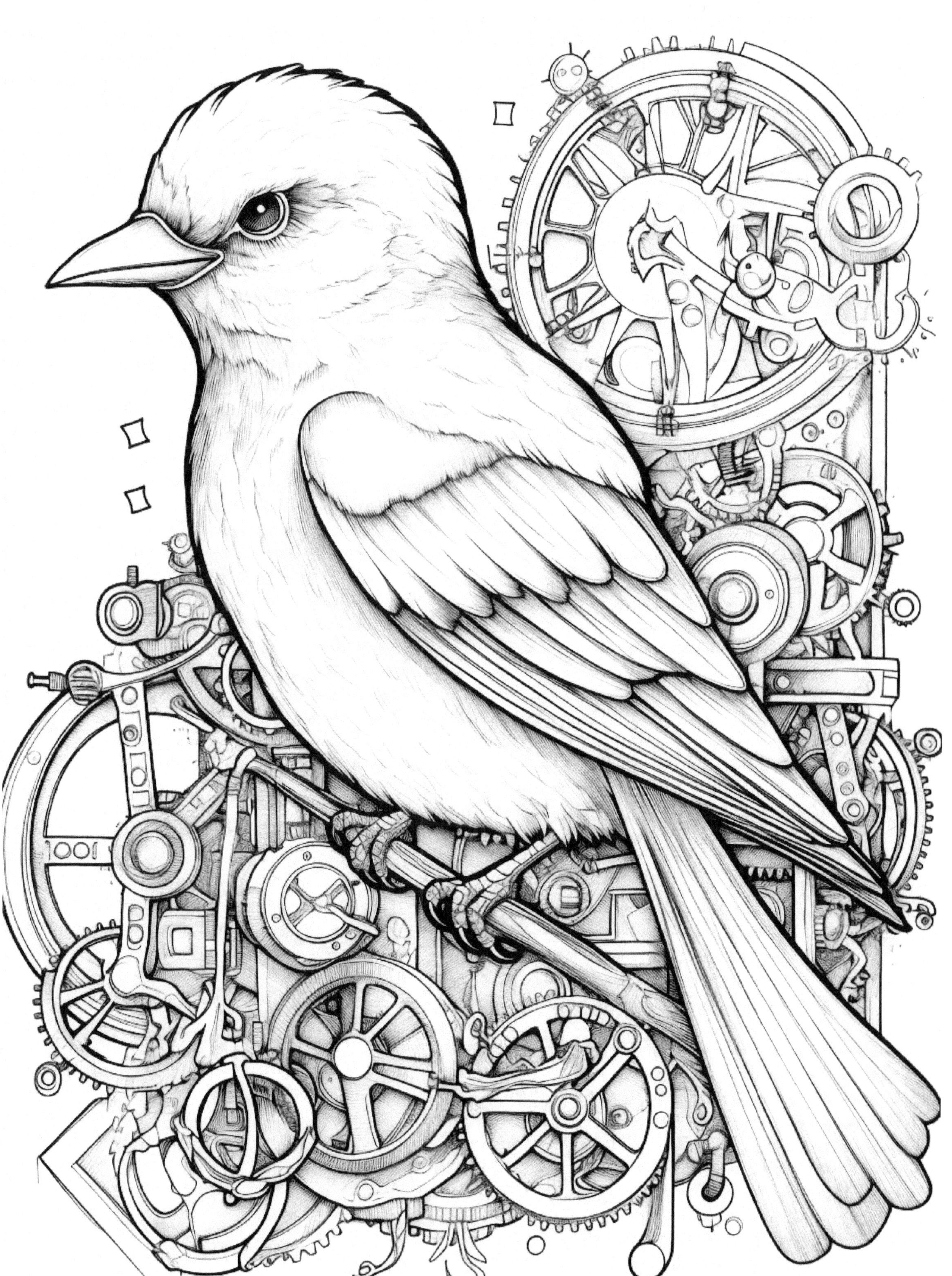

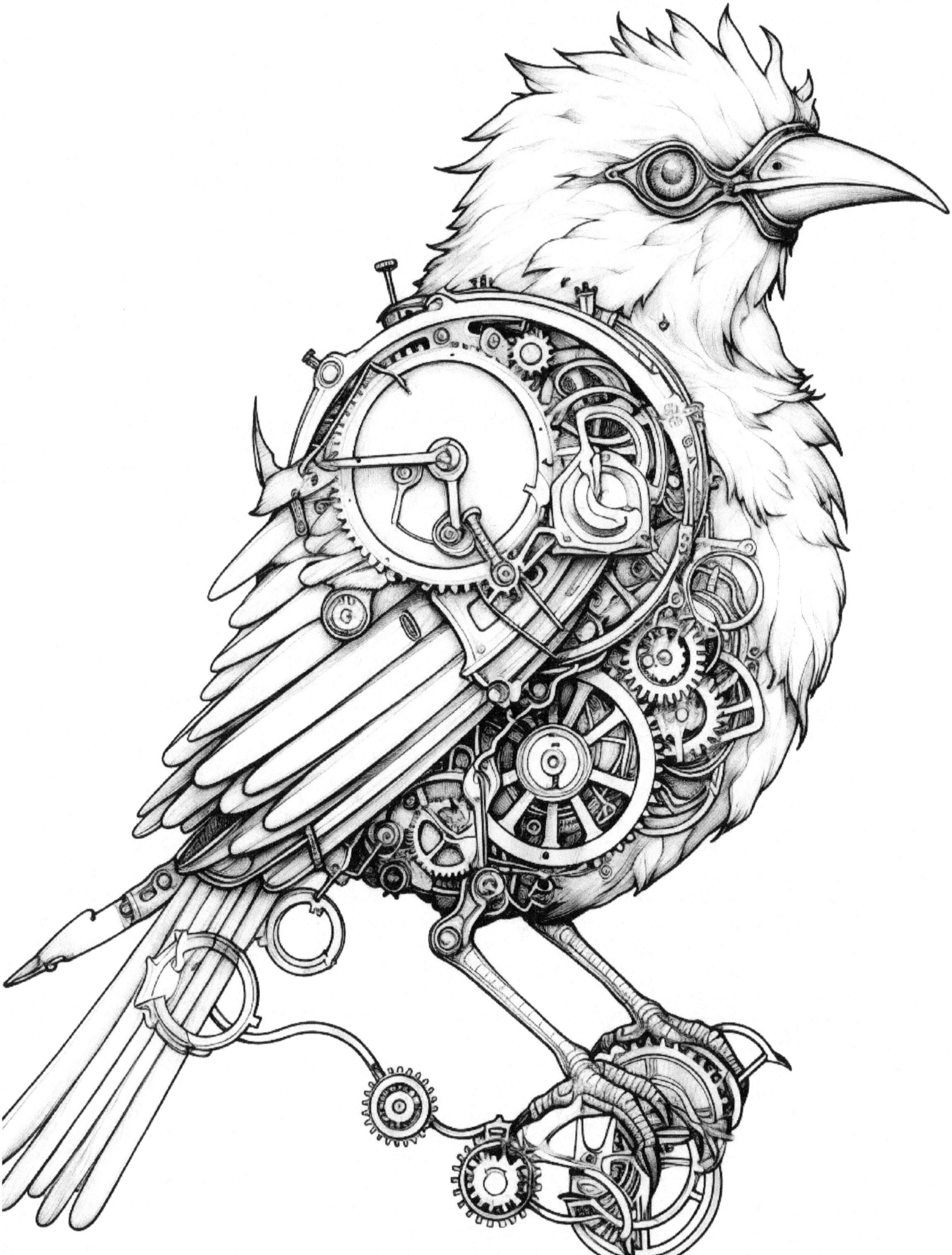

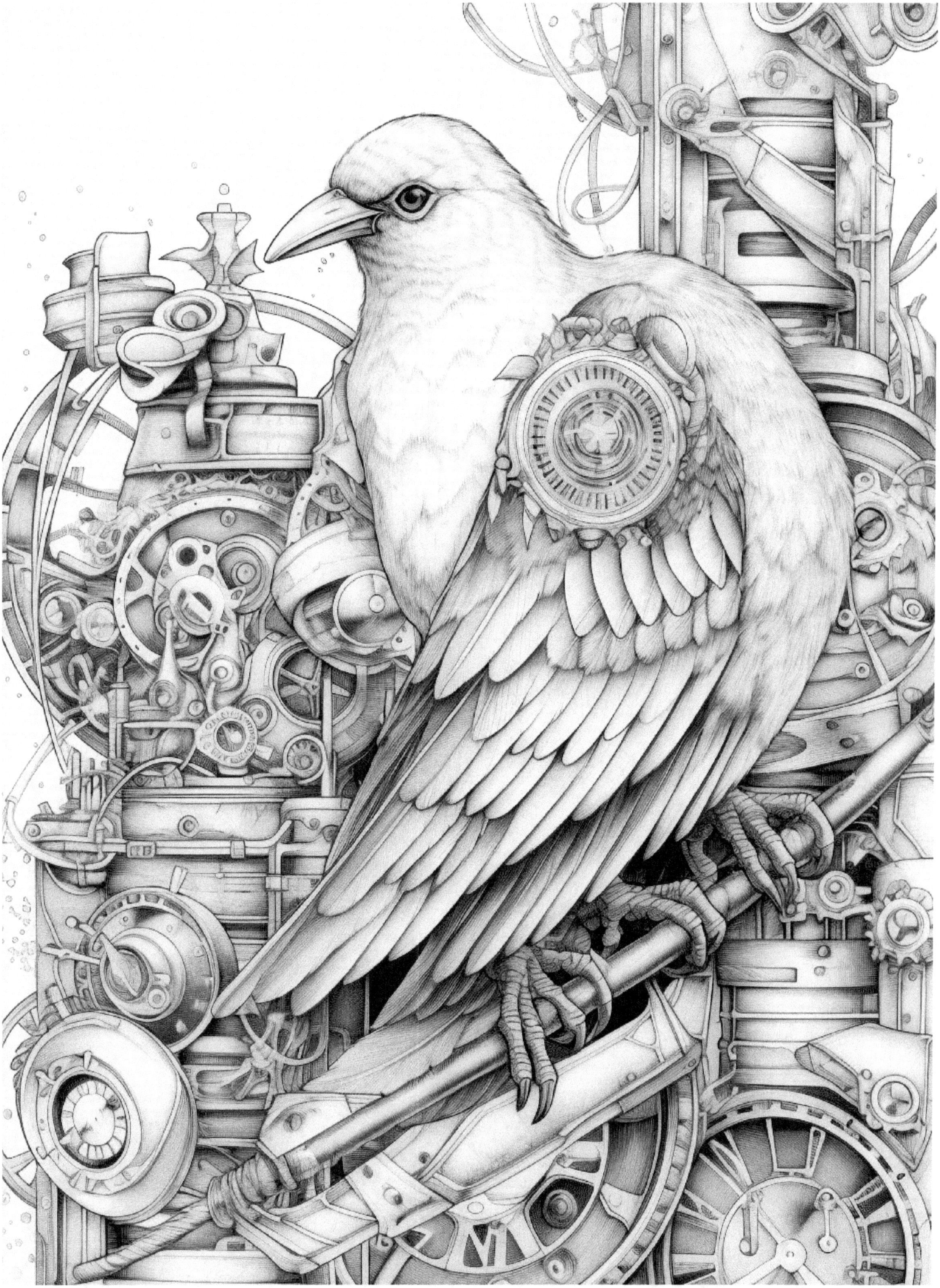

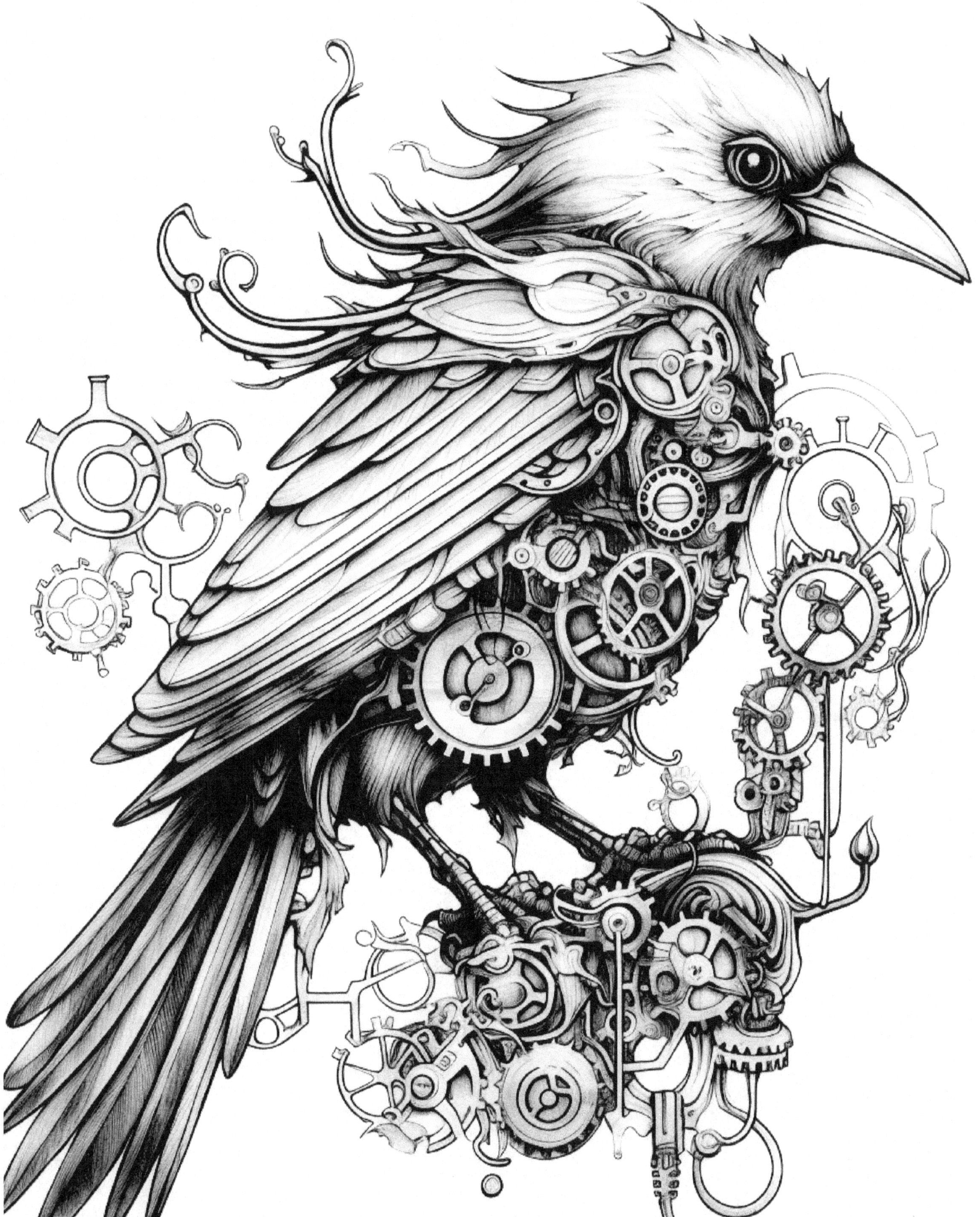

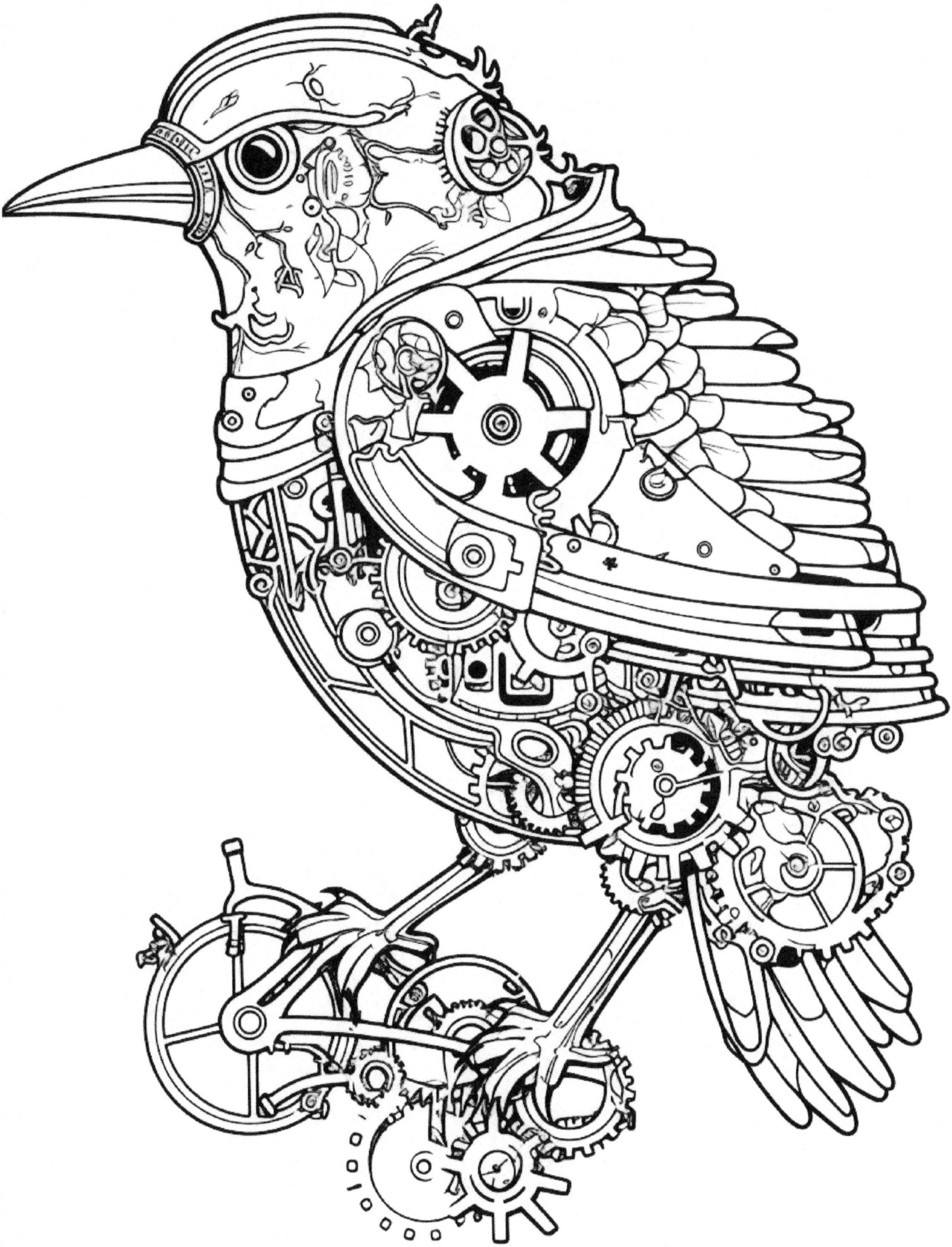

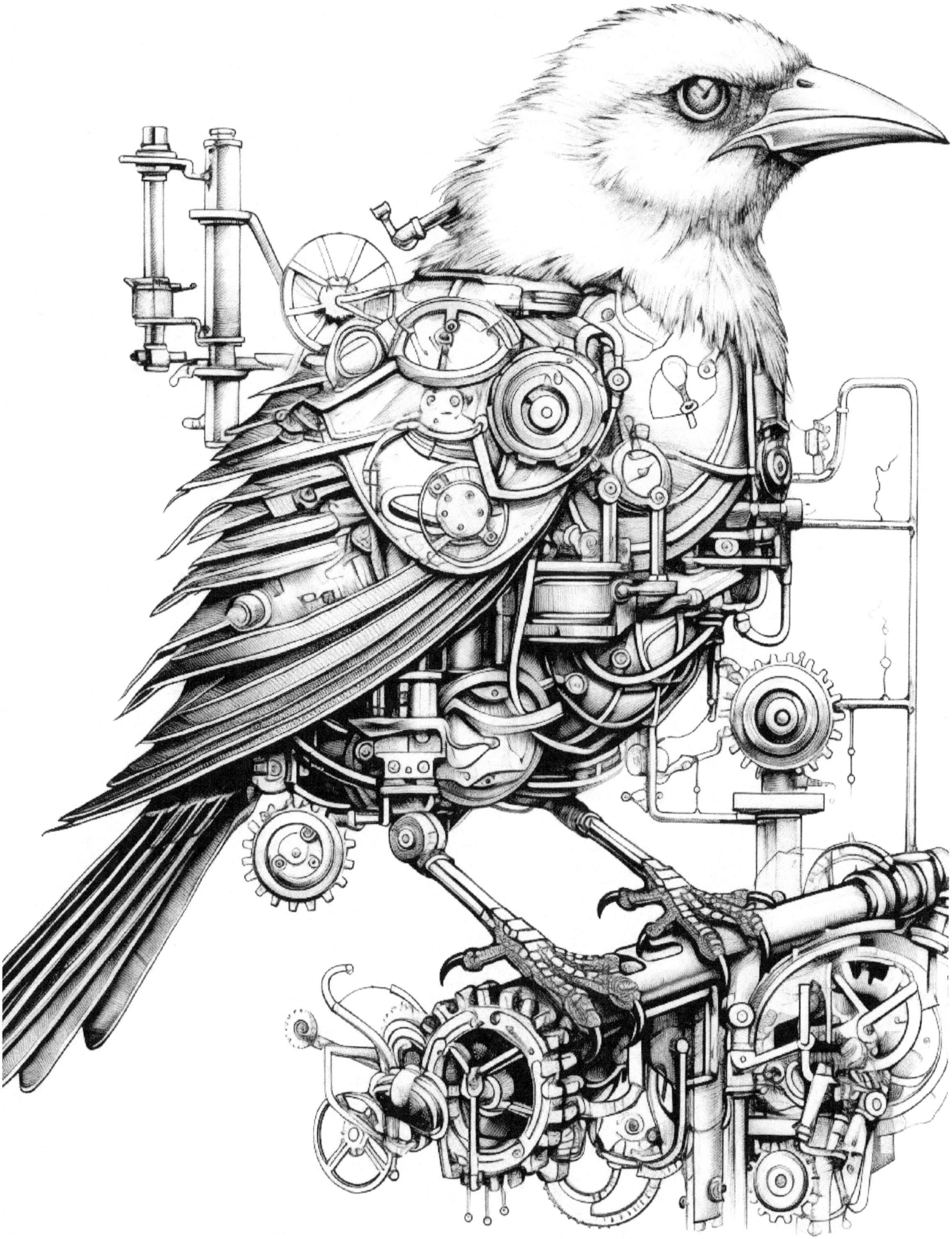

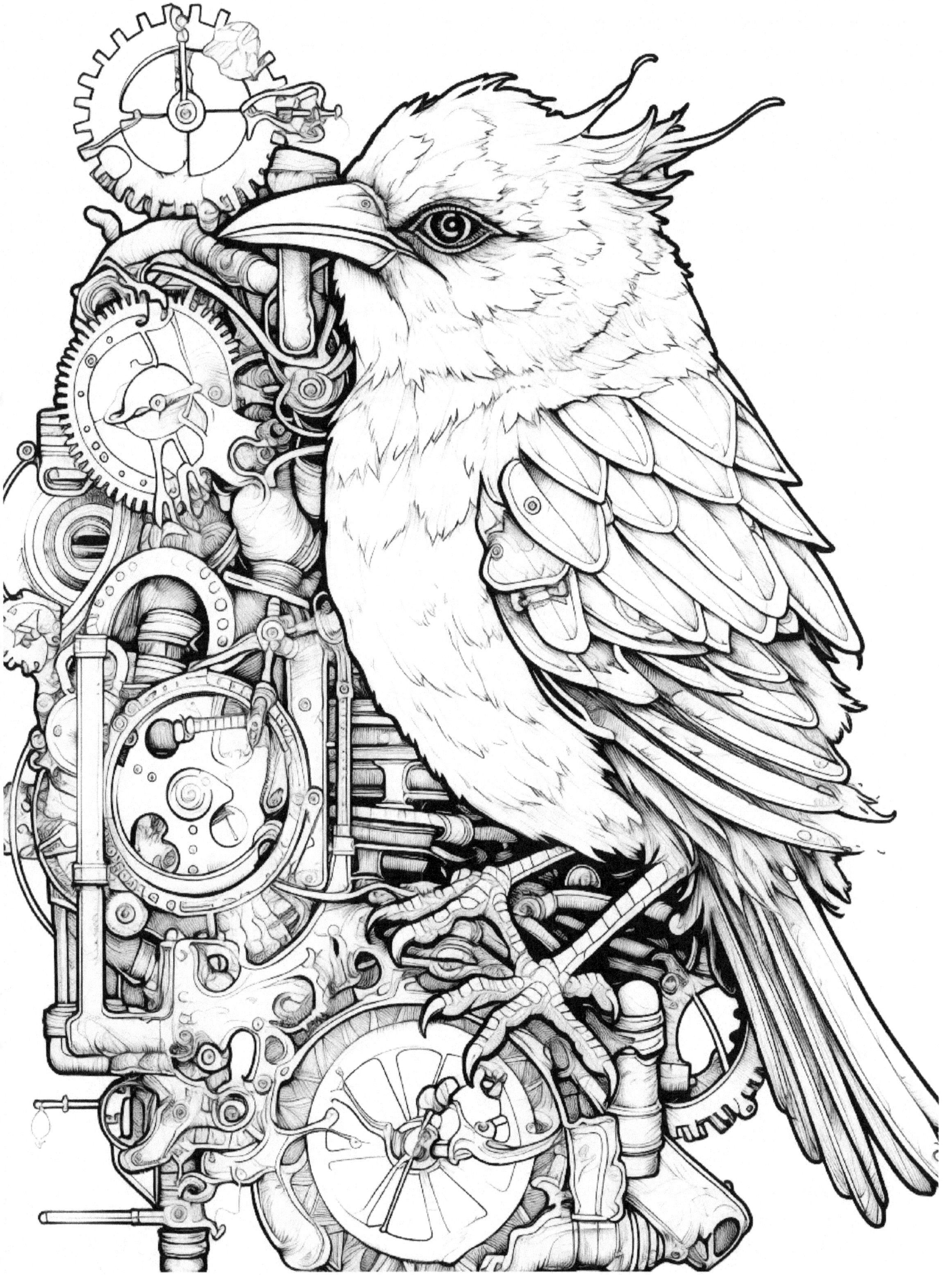

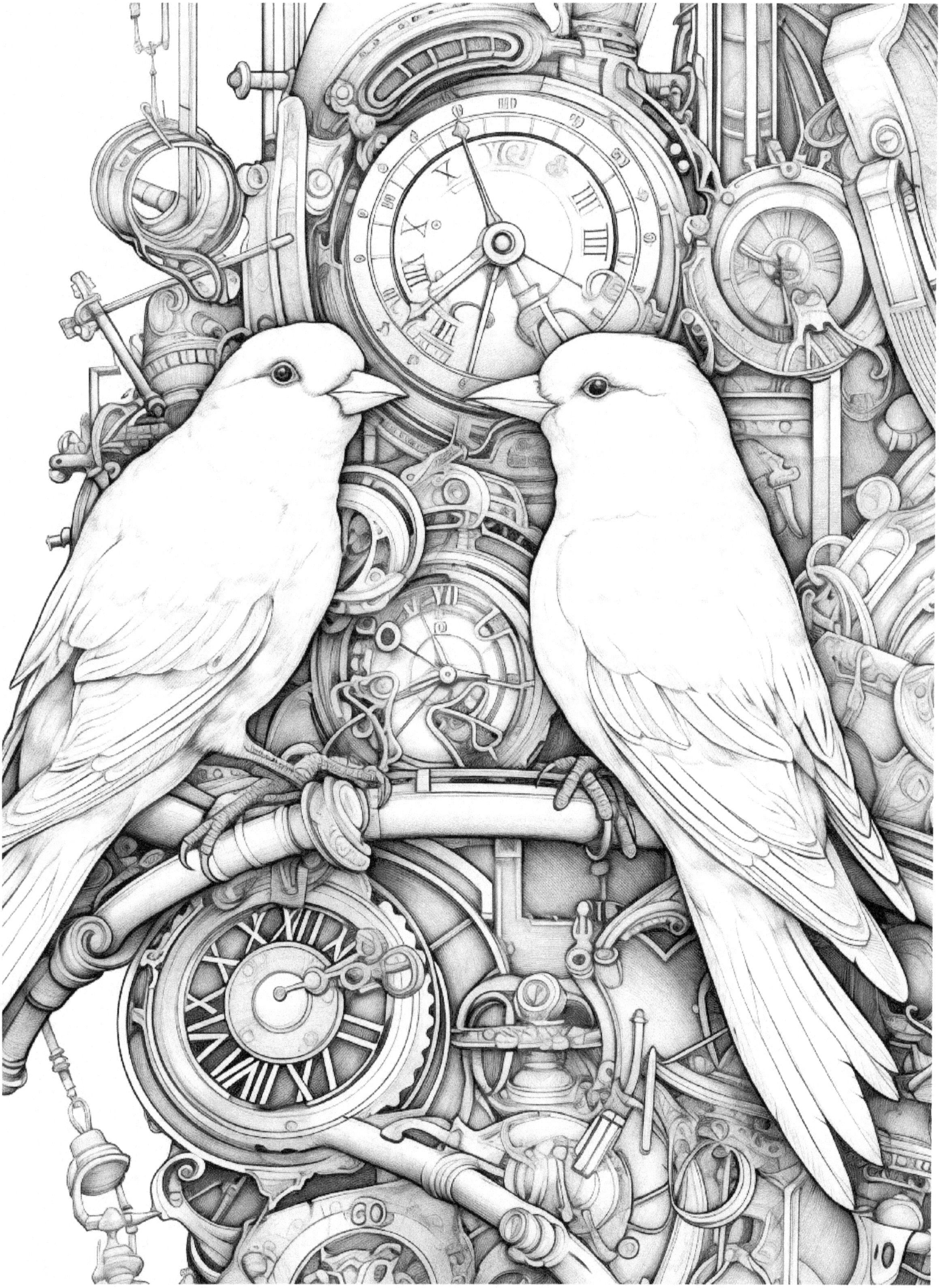

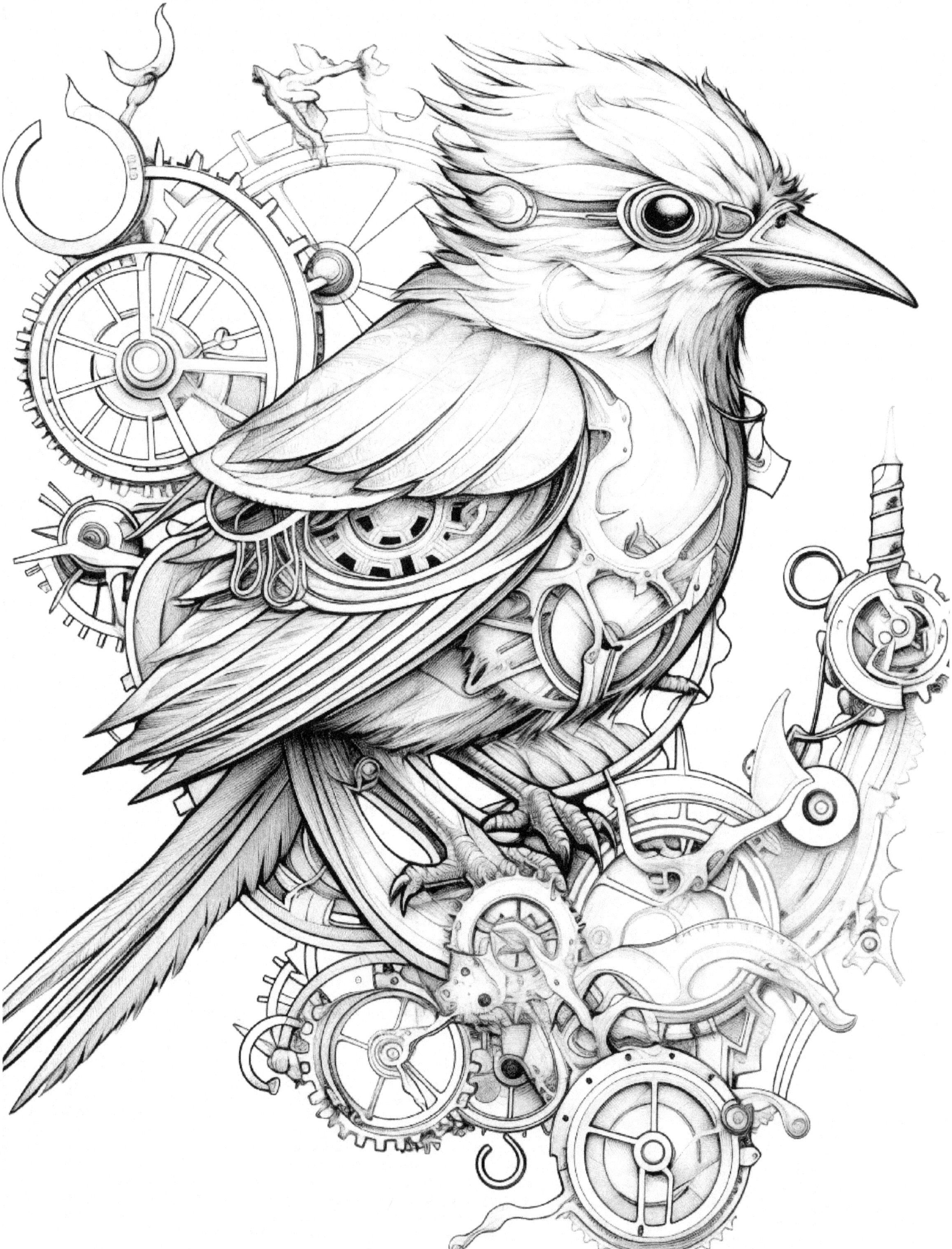

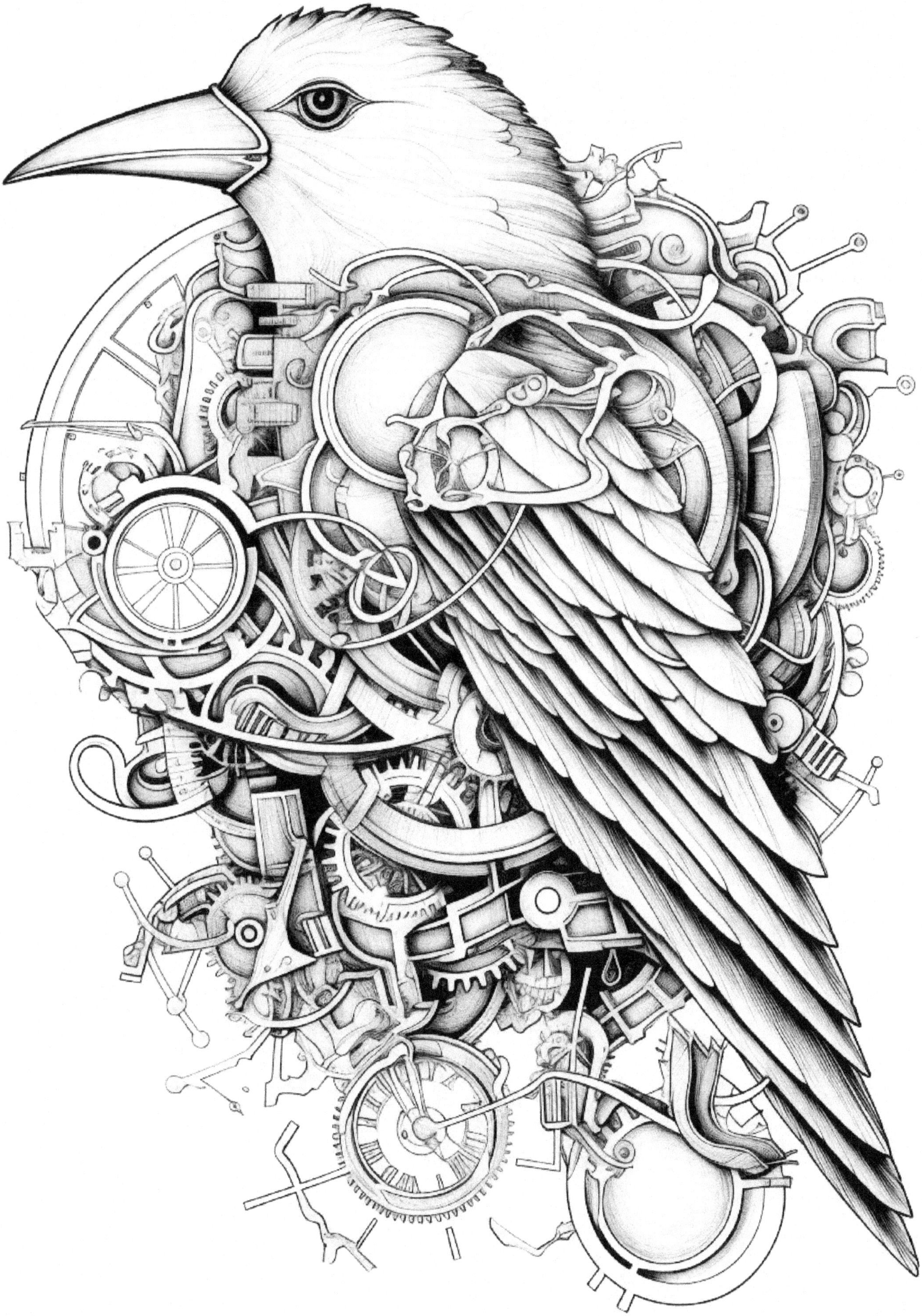

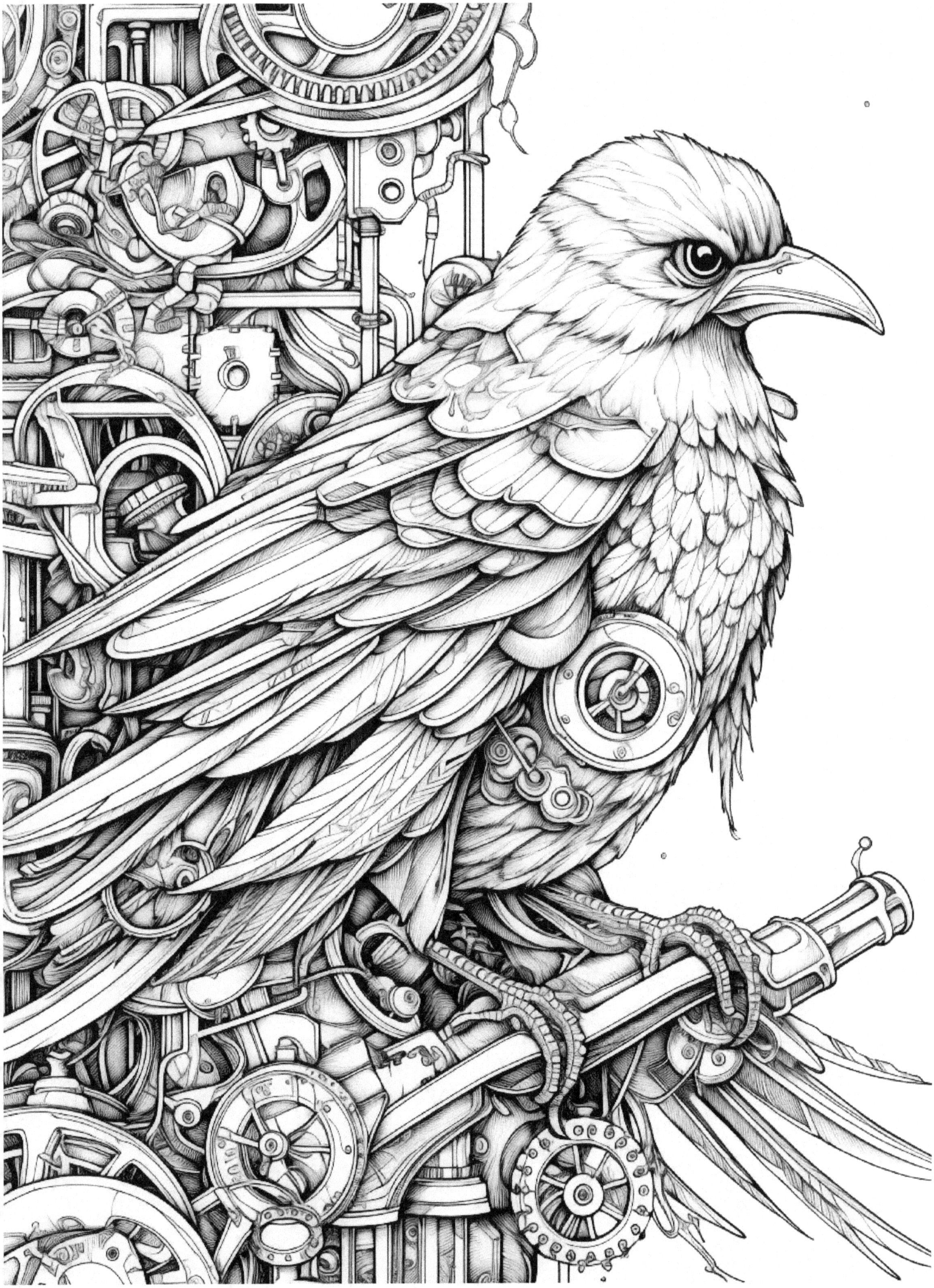

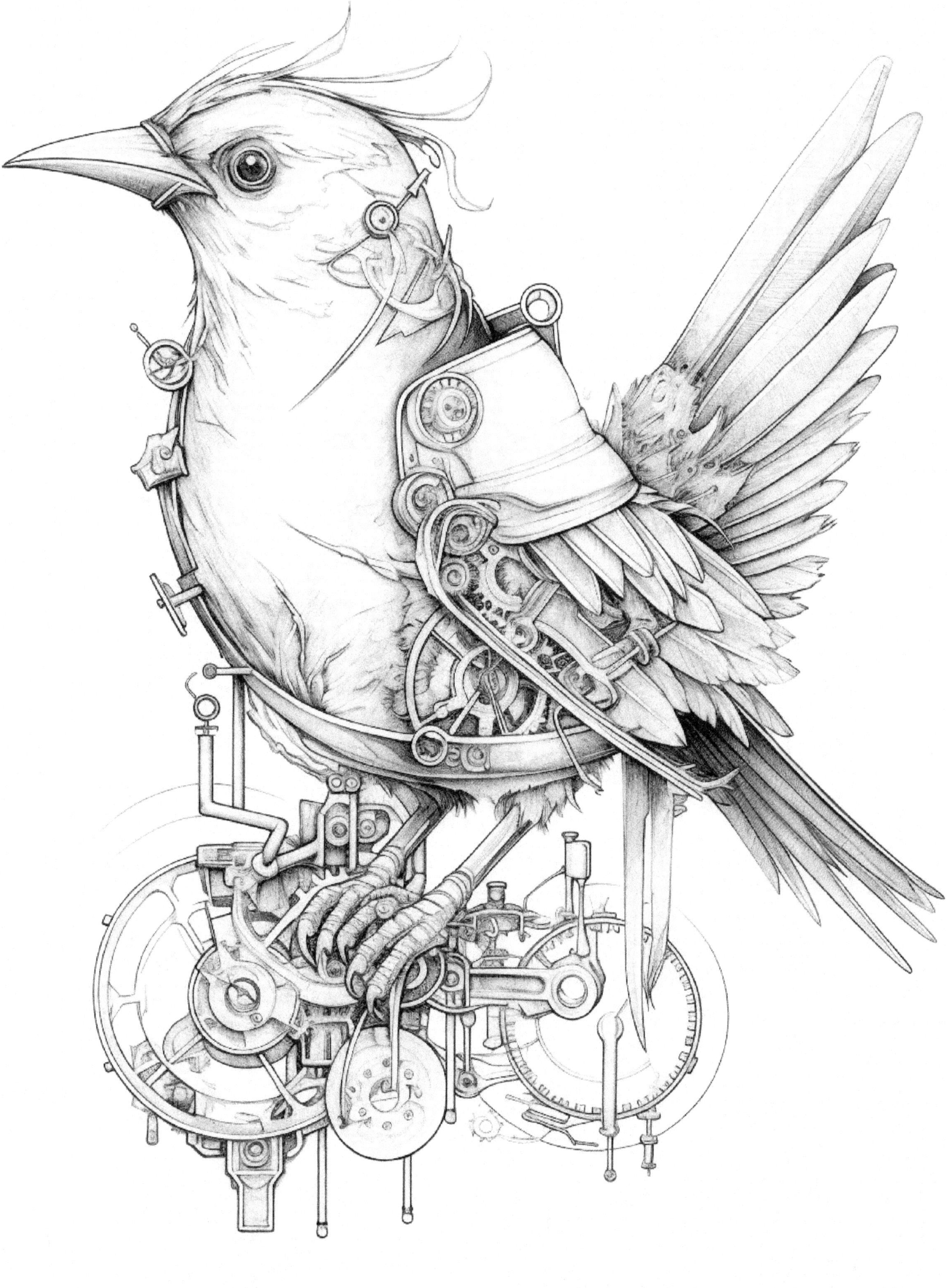

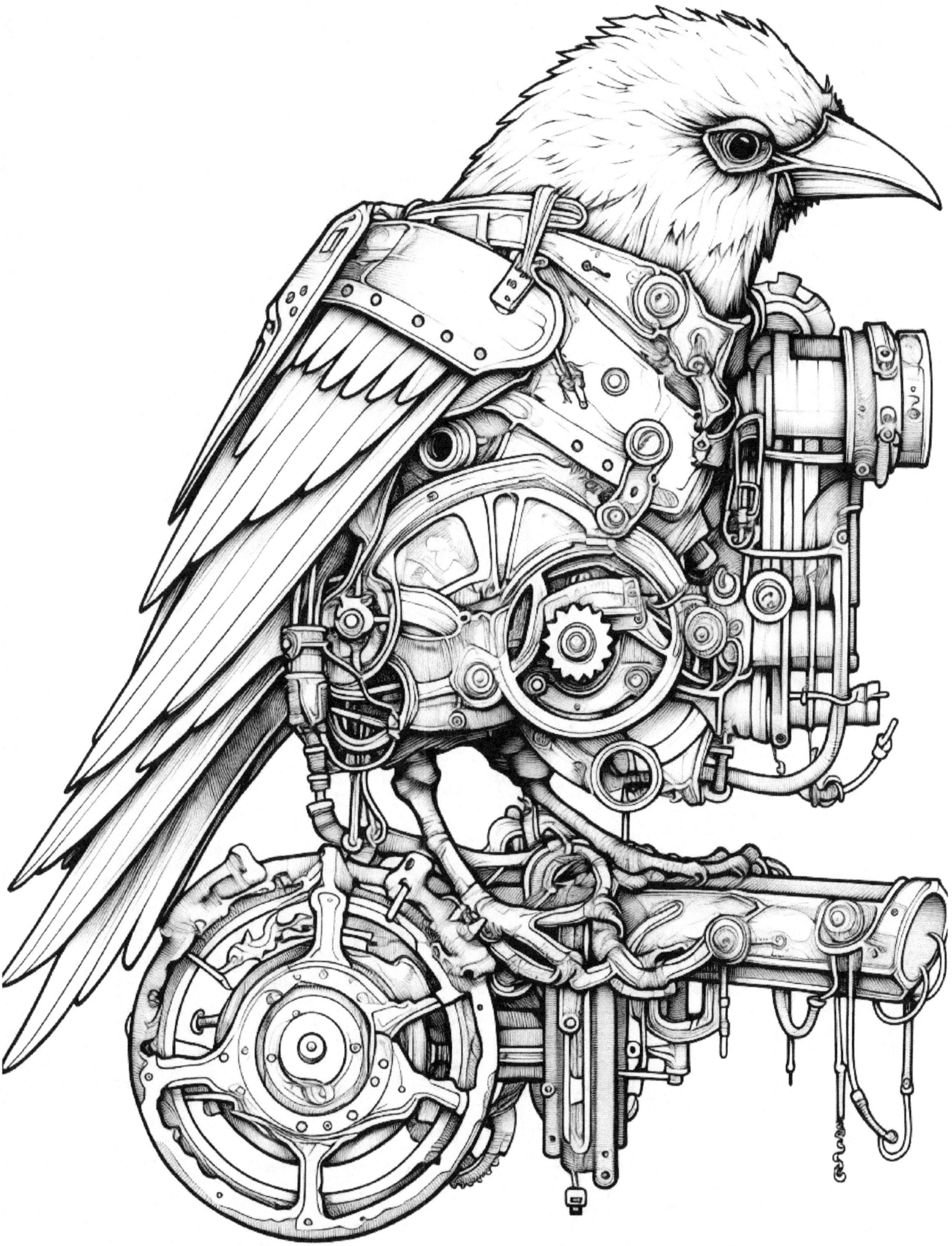

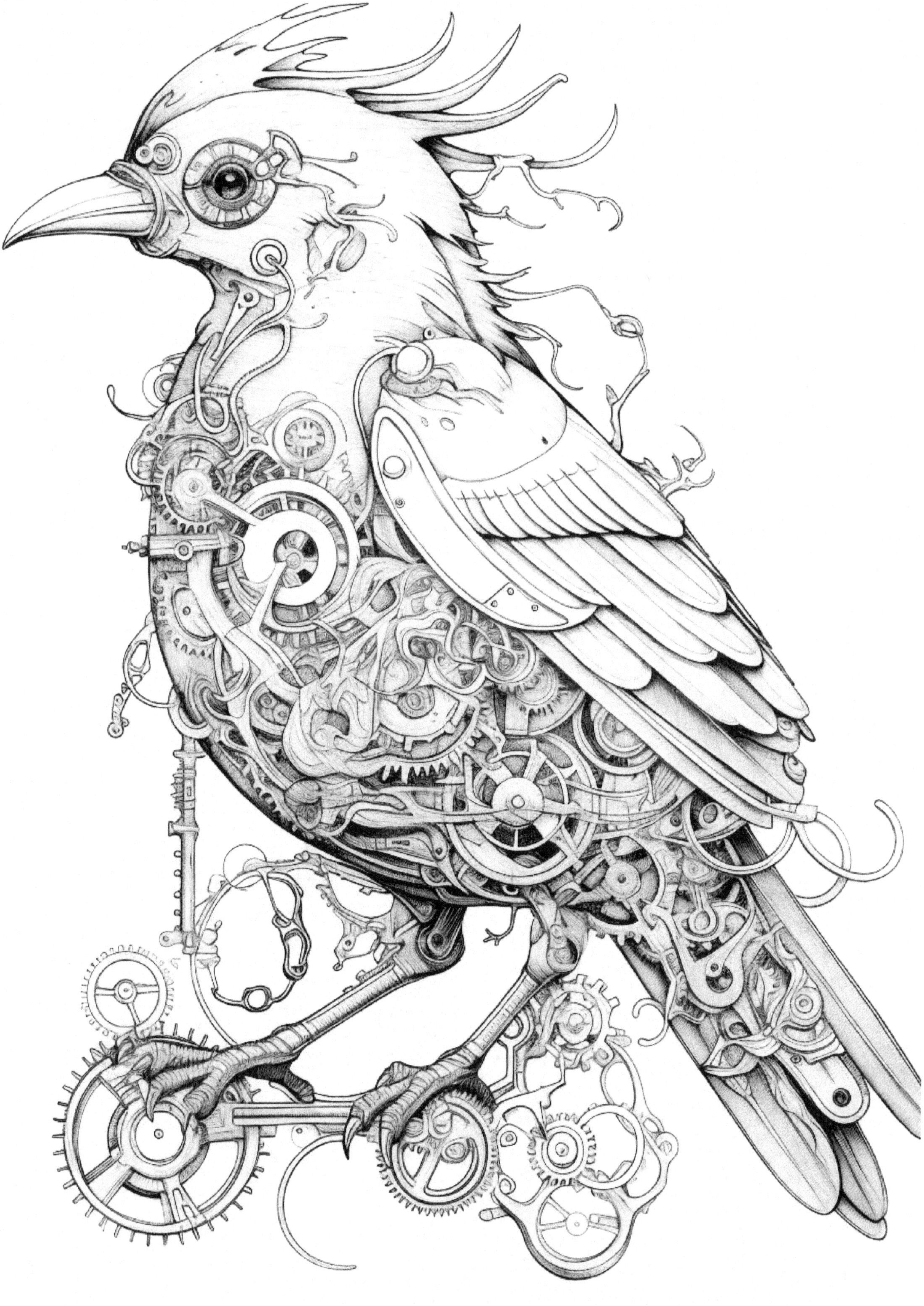

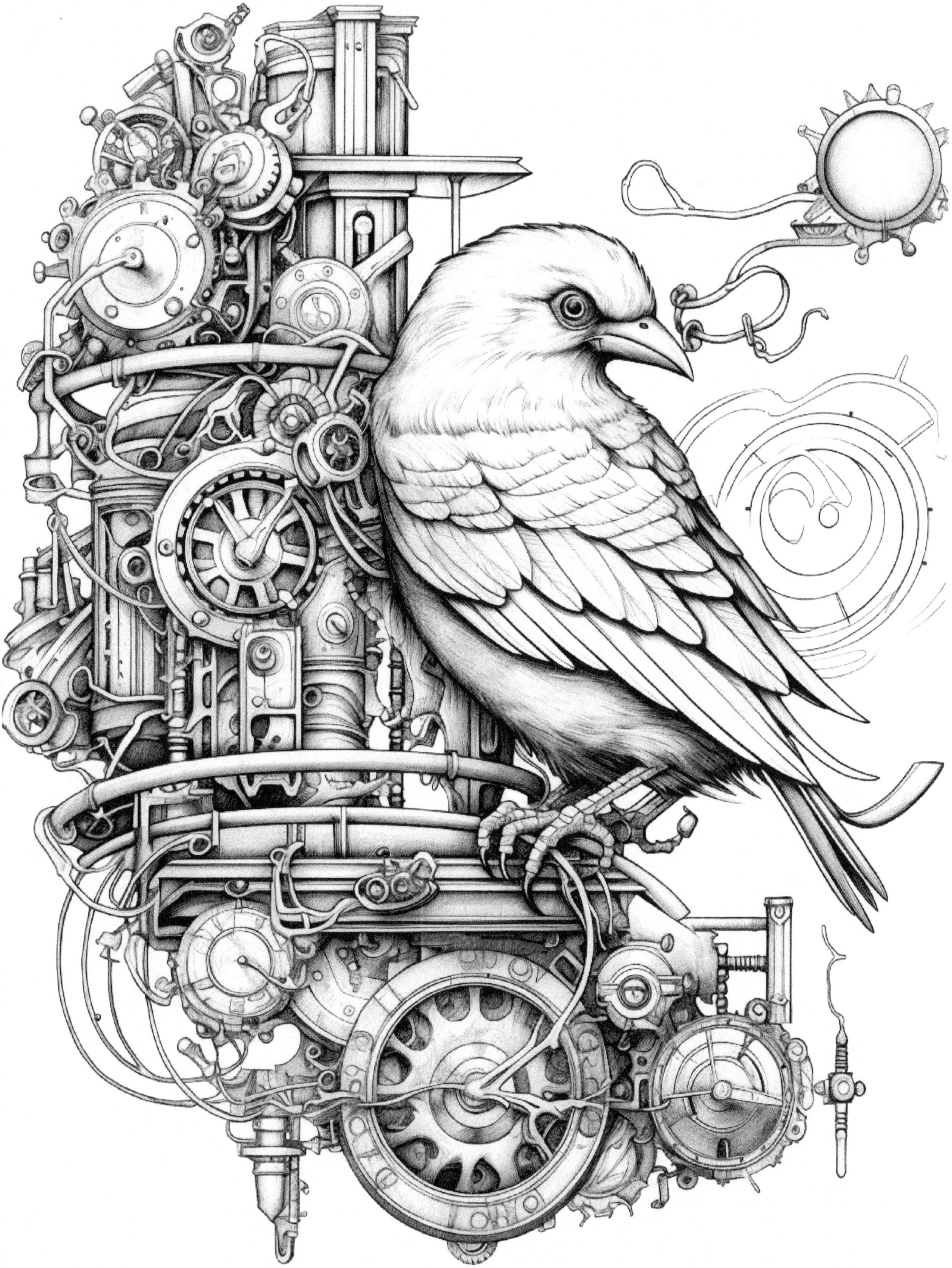

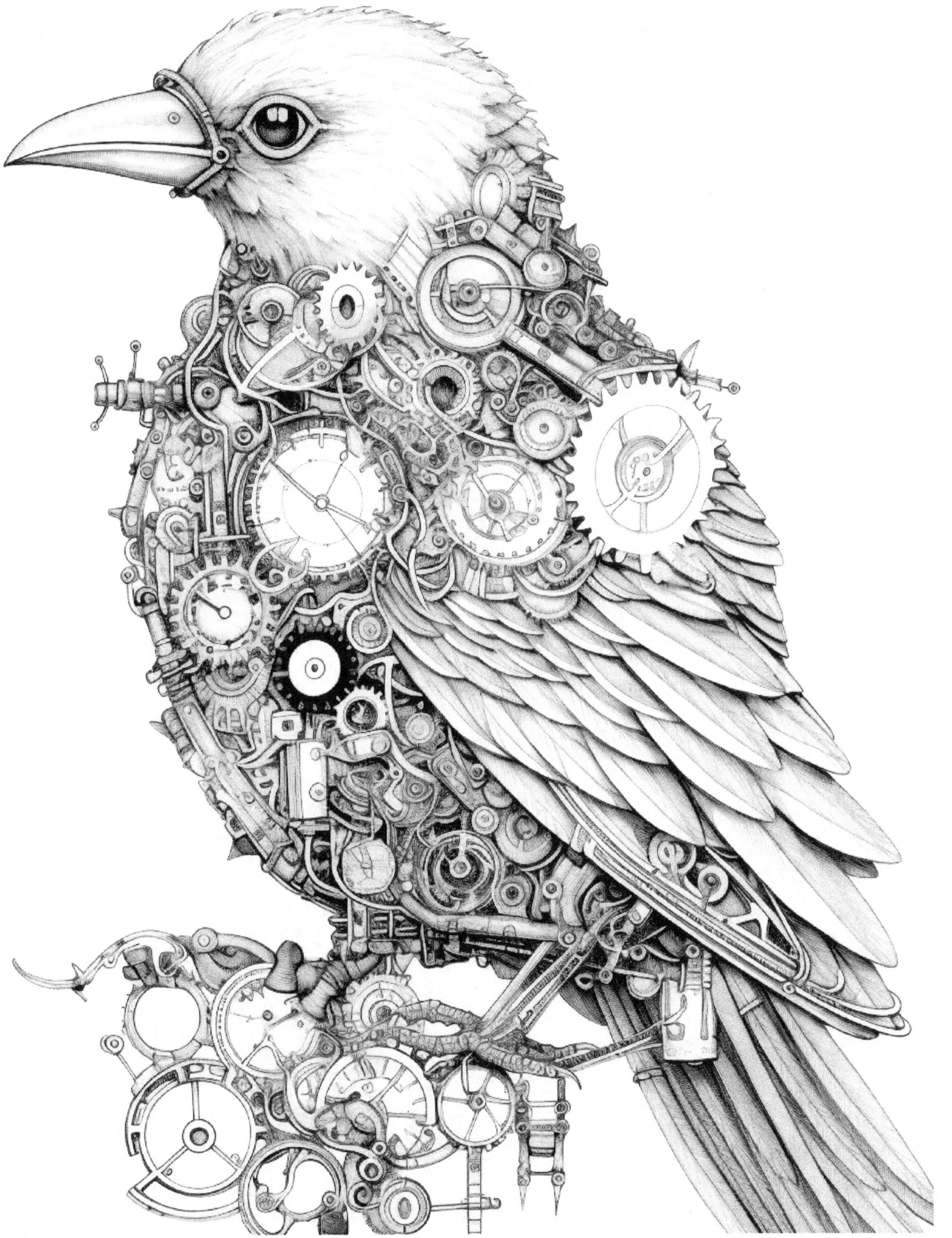

www.ingramcontent.com/pod-product-compliance
Lightning Source LLC
Chambersburg PA
CBHW082113220526
45472CB00009B/2158
9798328110235